DIVINE HEALING

THE WONDER AND THE MYSTERY

Compiled by Alison Chant

All scriptures in this book are from The New International Version unless otherwise stated

COPYRIGHT © 2006 ALISON CHANT

ALL RIGHTS RESERVED WORLDWIDE

ISBN 1-931178-20-8

Vision Publishing
1115 D Street Ramona, CA 92065
1-800-9-VISION
www.visionpublishingservices.com

CONTENTS

Preface   7

Foreword   9

Chapter One –   11
God is Able – A Bible Miracle Repeated; Hospitalisation Failed -But God Succeeded; God Gave Me a Voice to Praise Him; Angina Pectoris Completely Healed; Prayer removes Warts; Surgery Failed – Prayer Succeeded; Infected Eyes and Lungs Healed; A Miracle Only God Could Perform.

Chapter Two –   21
The Healing Ministry – Our First Testimony; Why is not everyone healed who follows this pattern? Hudson Taylor's Experience; Steps to Claiming the Promises.

Chapter Three –   29
The Ministry of Jesus – Characteristics of Jesus; A Variety of Method; What can we learn from these methods of Jesus? Do we need any special anointing to heal the sick? Healed of Endometriosis; The Sequel; Ken's Healing.

Chapter Four –   39
Do You Want To Get Well? – The Man at the Pool of Bethesda; More Mysteries; Why are some healed instantly and some not? Why are unbelievers sometimes healed? Does God expect more from Christians? Is it lack of faith? Why does God work more mightily in a new area? Missionaries Amazed; Boundaries to Healing.

Chapter Five –   51
Hindrances to Healing – Communion is Important; More hindrances; Finding More Answers; Concerning Chastening; Can Sickness Return; What about the climate of faith?

Chapter Six – 65
A Climate of Faith – Scottish Covenanters; Smith Wigglesworth; John Wesley's Healing; Barry Chant's Healing - A Horrible Shock; His Recovery Was Steady; Determined to Believe; Doctor Amazed; An Ongoing Miracle; More wonderful miracles.

Chapter Seven – 75
Three Keys to Faith – The Key of a Deep Desire; The Key of a Steady Determination; The Key of a Joyful Anticipation; Dr William Standish Reed's *'Surgery of the Soul'*.

Chapter Eight – 85
The Healing Covenant – Can we expect God to heal if we take no notice of his advice? Dr. Don Colbert's *'Toxic Relief';* Toward Health and Happiness; Extract's from James' Letter; Will God heal mental illness? Can Christians suffer emotional problems? What are some of the symptoms? Should we pray for them, or teach them, or both?

Chapter Nine – 97
More Wonderful Healings – This Sickness is Not Unto Death - Testimony from Stephen Dowling; A Mother's Faith; Paralysed, Blind and Dumb; A Sure Word From God; God Performs the Miracle; Doctors Amazed; Frank Holland's Testimony; Helen Leek's Testimony.

Chapter Ten – 109
A Journey to Wholeness – A Wonderful Healing–By a Fire of Gidgee Coals; God's Timing is Perfect; God Gets My Attention; Amazing Grace; Healed of a Blood Disease; Glossary of Terms.

Chapter Eleven – 121
Five Rules of Faith – God Only Answers the Prayer of Faith; You must believe that God is able; You must believe that God will; Believe that now is God's time to answer your prayer; Believe in the power of your own prayer; Make your prayer an active one.

Chapter Twelve – 129
A Finished Work - Testimony from Dorothy Woolf - Healed of Systemic Lupus Erythematosis, Devouring Scripture; The Law of the

Spirit of Life; God Requires Faith; My Decision; My Steps to Healing; A Copy of the Test Results.

Chapter Thirteen – 137
***All Things Are Possible*!** – Ken and Marjorie Tydeman, Marjorie's Testimony- That's Not Active Faith! Healed at Death's Door; Parents Asked to Repudiate Healing; Another Tumour in My Throat; A Period of Disobedience; Addicted to Morphine; A Terrible Accident; My Mother Cultivated a Vision! "She Will Live in Jesus Name!" Gangrene Healed; God Was Behind My Decision; My Struggles With God; Jesus Speaks to Me Through the Preacher; I Finally Give In to God; Jesus Promises Joy and Peace; Jesus Sets Me Free of the Morphine Addiction; My Leg Grows and I Rise Up and Walk; No More Blood Disease – I Am Completely Whole; Do Miracles Happen, Yes!

Chapter Fourteen – 163
God is Good - Thora Stands Up to Be Counted; Set Free From Mental Illness; June Can Sing Again; Myelin Sheath Restored to Nerve; Allergies Healed; Clubbed Feet Straightened; Arthritis Healed; Curvature of the Spine Straightened; Healed After Three Back Surgeries; Learning to Walk Again - Alan's Testimony; Scoliosis Healed; Cataract Removed Through Prayer.

Chapter Fifteen – 177
Healing Today - Healing Evangelism; Healing Rooms-Who is Chosen to Pray? One Caution from Johanna Michaelsen; Short Term Missions Trips; The Local Church.

Chapter Sixteen – 185
Conclusions – Sickness Called Discipline; Much Wisdom is Needed; A Realm of Faith! A Challenge!

Appendix 193

Bibliography 195

The Wonder and the Mystery of Divine Healing
Alison Chant

PREFACE

For years I have puzzled over the reason why more people are not able to grasp God's healing promise. To gain understanding I began to gather testimonies of healing in an endeavour to pierce the mystery that seemed to me to surround the healing ministry. Slowly but surely I obtained the answers to many of the questions I had asked myself. This book is the result of my searching.

I realise and appreciate that mighty men and women of faith with a great understanding of the healing gift have written books on the subject of healing. So why another book?

This particular book not only gives some answers to my many questions, it is also a celebration of some of the wonderful things God has done over the past generation of believing faith. My prayer is that this book, *Divine Healing -The Wonder and the Mystery* will inspire some of the new generation of Christian men and women to seek the Lord earnestly for the gift of faith, gifts of healing, and the working of miracles. (1 Co 12:8-11) It is the demonstration of these gifts which will galvanise the world to sit up and take notice that there is a God, that he is a healing God, and that he rewards those who diligently seek him. The Lord who, through the apostle Paul, has told us to desire earnestly all the spiritual gifts (1 Co 14:1) will surely answer the heart cry of those who feel led to seek those gifts that are needed to bring healing to the suffering of this generation.

My thanks to all those who have provided testimonies to share, especially Ken and Marjorie Tydeman; Stephen Dowling; Dorothy Woolf; Frank Holland; Helen Leek; and Tex Quicksilver, Thanks also to Austin Hudson for preserving and making available testimonies from his history of the CRC church in Tasmania where Ken and I worked for sixteen years.

And finally my grateful thanks to my husband, Ken Chant, Barry Chant, and Stan DeKoven for their useful insights that have helped in the writing of this book.

Alison Chant

The Wonder and the Mystery of Divine Healing
Alison Chant

FOREWORD

Alison Chant has written a real gem of a book in what follows. I have been really stirred by its content and challenged afresh to reach out for the gifts of healing and miracles.

Jesus once said to a group of Sadducees, *"You are in error, for you know neither the word nor the power of God."* This book makes no such error. It is strong in teaching and uses the Scripture to establish the biblical basis for the ministries of healing and miracles and at the same time answers most of the questions that people have in these areas, especially when things don't turn out as they expected or prayed. It is also strong in the power of God, for it quotes testimony after testimony of the marvellous things that God has done. Not only are there dozens of remarkable validated stories from many sources, but Alison also shares her own experience of God's healing power which is equally remarkable. This makes reading this book both enlightening and gripping. You will not be able to put it down.

I suppose Alison's hope is that through the message of this book, you will become bolder to use the Gifts of the Spirit and see the wonderful healings and miracles that God makes possible to all who believe. The book creates a momentum in your heart which results in a wave of faith to help you deal with all the doubts and fears that can cross your mind as you observe, and then deal with, the real suffering that many people endure. I trust that you are challenged as you read, as indeed I have been.

Ray Gilmour
Pastor
Christian Family Centre
Pukekohe New Zealand

The Wonder and the Mystery of Divine Healing
Alison Chant

CHAPTER ONE

GOD IS ABLE

Jesus said, *"According to your faith will it be done to you"* (Mt 9:29) and it seems without doubt that believing faith is the foundation for the healing miracles God has promised in his Word.

During fifty three years of ministry together my husband, Ken, and I have seen many remarkable answers to prayer. However there were other times when we expected a healing to take place but were disappointed. Indeed, over those same years, we observed Christians of world renown, desperately sick, who were earnestly prayed for by many thousands yet were not healed.

Because of these failures in realising the healing promise we finally came to understand that God is Sovereign and for some reason, known only to him, he sometimes withholds the healing or the miracle desired. Here is a mystery we cannot fathom. However, that does not mean we should abandon the healing message. Far from it! In these pages I would like to introduce you to many wonderful healing miracles and to reveal a little of the wonder and the mystery of divine healing, and of the promise of God

Through the years '63-'69 we experienced a wave of divine healing in our church in Launceston Tasmania. It was a time of great blessing yet there remained for us many mysteries, things we found hard to understand.

Over those years of blessing, healing was preached constantly yet some people for whom we prayed were not healed and some died of their illness. Despite this Ken continued to preach healing even when, especially when, the apparent failures occurred. He maintained that God's promise that healing was available was still true, even though we did not always see a successful conclusion to our prayers.

Now, many years later, with a greater understanding of the healing promise, we can see some reasons why those prayers, even though prayed with great earnestness, did not always bring us the victory for which we so greatly yearned.

The victories that were achieved were tremendous as the testimonies in this chapter reveal. There were many more healings than we have room to tell here. [1]

Surgery Failed – Prayer Succeeded

Fifteen years ago I had a double tooth extraction which left a puncture through my gum and jawbone and into the antrum. This perforation was discovered when I rinsed my mouth with water, because the water trickled into my nose. The dentist expected the hole to heal naturally, but it didn't, and eventually it became infected and painful.

I received various kinds of (unsuccessful) treatment, culminating in an operation to place a

---

[1] Excerpts from the magazine <u>Revivalist</u> August 1963 & March 1969

plastic flap over the decayed bone. This proved unsatisfactory and another operation was needed to put a drainage hole at the back of my nose. However after twelve months this hole closed, necessitating yet another operation. But this too failed and my mouth remained infected and painful.

Then one Sunday night Pastor Chant (who did not know of my problem) said he felt impressed by the Lord to pray for someone with an infected sore in the roof of the mouth. I indicated that I was probably the person concerned, and the Pastor prayed for me.

Within a short time all trace of the trouble left me, and my dentist has confirmed that the hole has closed and the infection is gone. Praise God for his divine power. (*H. J. Harvey*)

A Bible Miracle Repeated

I have a testimony very much like the man with the withered hand, who stretched out his hand when Jesus told him to and was healed. Some nine months ago I was faced with an operation on my right hand; the muscles were all tight and I was unable to sew or write or do anything else that required the use of my fingers. The doctors recommended cutting the tendons in the hand to loosen the fingers and muscles.

But one Sunday night, as he was praying for the people, Pastor Chant said he believed the Lord had shown him there was someone in the congregation who had an affliction in the muscles of the right hand, and asked the person to lift their hand for prayer.

I raised my hand and explained my condition, and as I sat there with my hand uplifted, the pastor prayed for me. Instantly the Lord healed me, and on the way out after the service I was able to shake hands vigorously with the people! Since then my hand has been quite well, and I am able to use it normally. *(D. E. French)*

Hospitalisation Failed – But God Succeeded

For nearly twelve years I suffered greatly from a diseased gall bladder. I was hospitalised for treatment but was not cured. Time and again I had to walk the floor at night, because of the severe pain, and there were many things I was unable to eat. Three doctors X-rayed me and told me that only an operation to remove the gall bladder would bring me any relief.

However, about nine months ago I stepped out into the prayer line and asked Pastor Chant to lay hands on me and pray for God to heal me. From that time on the pain and sickness disappeared, and now I have no need of an operation. Proof of my healing is that now I can eat anything I like without the least discomfort!

Also I suffered from sinusitis for over eighteen months, and this too caused me real pain and distress. About five months ago I asked for prayer for this and once again the Lord wonderfully healed me. Now there is no trace of either of these diseases in my body.

I do thank God for saving my soul, for leading me through the waters of baptism into a new and wonderful life, for baptising me in the Holy Spirit, and for filling my days with his rich love and happiness. (*C. M. Hayes*)

God Gave Me a Voice to Praise Him

For many years I suffered repeatedly from a throat condition that was always present with me, but especially after times of stress it would flare up, become very sore and cause ulceration and loss of my voice. All medical efforts failed to clear up this infection, and many doctors said that only surgery could help me.

However, for one reason or another I did not enter hospital, and felt that God was restraining me from the operation. Then last year I felt I should cease all treatment and just let the Lord take over completely. I asked Pastor Chant to pray for my healing, and then stood firmly on the promise of God, believing that he would heal me.

For a week or two the condition seemed to worsen, but I had an inner confidence that the Lord was undertaking, and that the Father's healing was being accomplished. And so it was, for in a short time our miracle-working Father completely healed me! Once again he proved that miracles are for our day, and that all we have to do is have unwavering faith in his Word. I do thank the Lord for the health and happiness I now enjoy all the time. Thank you Father! (*Eileen A. Hawke*)

Angina Pectoris Completely Healed

I would like to tell you about the wonderful healing I have received from God. Some four years ago I was stricken with pains in the chest and arms and decided to visit a doctor. I explained my symptoms to him, and a cardiograph was taken which revealed that I had angina pectoris. The doctor warned me not to lift anything heavy, and to always walk slowly. He prescribed some tablets, also some to place under my tongue when in pain. After two years on this treatment I found my condition becoming worse. I couldn't walk briskly for twenty-five yards without pain.

Then a friend advised me to go to pastor Chant at the CRC. He told me they prayed for the sick. So I decided to attend their services, and one Sunday night I went out for prayer. I felt improvement, but slipped back to my previous condition. I decided to try again. This was in August of last year. Once again I improved slightly after prayer. However the September issue of the Revivalist was out, and in that issue I read an article written by a retired Methodist minister (Rev. D. T. Reddin). He described in the article three kinds of faith – historic faith, temporary faith, and active faith. He said people with temporary faith are those who go out for prayer, feel improvement, and then when a test of faith comes through a return of their symptoms, they fade out, instead of matching the challenge with a more determined prayer of faith.

I realised then that it was I who had to act in faith. So I took Mr. Reddin's advice and continually prayed for healing, determined to get healing through the power of God. The result was I started to improve. I found I could walk miles, and even run, without pain. Now I am back to normal. I can chop wood, and dig my garden without suffering any pain.

I thank God every day for the wonderful miracle I have received through his mighty healing power. *(Stan J. Shipp)*

Prayer Removes Warts

For nearly two years I was afflicted with warts on my left hand. These caused me a lot of trouble, and sometimes severe pain, and my hand was always sore. No treatment was successful, the warts continued to appear, and it seemed as if nothing could remove them. Then one Sunday night I asked pastor Chant to pray for my hand, and within two weeks every wart was gone, the scars were all healed, and scarcely any mark was left on my hand. Since that time I have not had the least discomfort in my hand, nor has there been any sign of the warts returning. Praise God for the power of prayer. *(Marion Henry)*

Infected Eyes and Lungs Healed

For three years I suffered with a very bad infection in my

eyes, and throughout that time I was not able to gain any relief from the drops and ointment given to me by the eye specialist. Then twelve months ago in the CRC meeting in Launceston I asked Pastor Chant to pray for me. The next day my eyes were much better, and during that week they were completely healed. How wonderful to be rid of that wretched infection!

Also, just over six years ago I contracted a severe illness in my lungs and spent some time in hospital. After this I was never free of pain in my left lung. Sometimes it was almost unbearable. Having put up with this for all those years, some four months ago I went out for prayer again, knowing in my heart that I was going to get rid of that pain. Well that's just what happened. I haven't had any sign of the pain since then, and I thank my Lord every day over and over again! Praise the Lord for his wonderful goodness and mercy to me. (B. Connors)

A Miracle Only God Could Perform

When I was nineteen years of age X-ray examination showed that I was suffering from a hole in my heart. Over the years this condition caused me much pain and misery, and I was told that only an operation would bring me any relief. Every two or three months I would suffer a severe blackout, and would have to spend three or four days in bed. The whole condition left me weak and exhausted, and greatly hindered my enjoyment of life, and interrupted my work.

But nine months ago my husband and I both attended the Crusade meetings in Launceston, and accepted Christ as our Saviour. Later on we were both baptized, and I asked Pastor Chant to pray for my healing. The power of God moved on me in a wonderful way, and I was instantly healed. That was over six months ago, and I have not suffered the least discomfort from my heart in all that time.

Along with my heart condition, I also suffered from a perforated eardrum. This made me practically deaf in one ear, and caused me very great pain if any water got into the ear, and also made me very dizzy and faint when I was travelling in a car over a high hill. However, since prayer (although doctors have told me it is impossible) I can hear perfectly, water no longer causes me any pain, and heights no longer make me dizzy!

Praise God for his wonderful and overflowing blessings! (*Vicki Beaumont*)

Vicki Beaumont, a Russian countess in her own right, lives now in New Zealand with her husband. Ken visited her some years ago and she was still rejoicing in her healing and praising God for his goodness.

These testimonies were the background needed for Ken to write his books on faith – *Faith Dynamics* and *Throne Rights* – that contain teaching on how to receive your miracle from God. Our whole life took a new direction from '78 as Ken was no longer a Pastor but instead a Bible College Principal. He had to make a conscious decision to let others continue with preaching the healing message while he spent the bulk of his time writing and teaching the whole counsel of God.

In the following chapters I will endeavour to explore the mystery of divine healing and cite more examples of God's healing power and the things we learned along the way.

CHAPTER TWO

THE HEALING MINISTRY

Our First Testimony

During 1955, in our very first church in Ballarat, Victoria, a woman named Mrs. Aitcheson came to us crippled with arthritis, in great pain, and unable to care for her home. She asked for prayer. There was no immediate sign of healing after she was anointed with oil and prayers were offered, but the very next day when Ken called to see how she was he was greeted by a radiant lady, with mop in one hand and bucket in the other. She was completely healed and cleaning her home from top to bottom! Her healing was the very first fruit that we saw of our healing ministry. We believed, we prayed, and God answered. Mrs. Aitcheson became our pianist for the church and faithfully played for us for many years.[2]

As depicted in chapter one, *God is Able,* we have experienced God's power to heal many times, yet not all

---

[2] Sometime later the Lord gave Mrs. Aitcheson another miracle, though this time it did not involve healing. She gave a message in tongues one Sunday during communion and on that particular Sunday we had a visitor. He was a professor of Hebrew from a Melbourne College. He came to us after the service and asked where Mrs. Aitcheson had learned the Hebrew language. Of course we told him she had not, but that she was using the gift of tongues! We were thrilled to hear that the interpretation given, though not a definitive translation nevertheless had given the message accurately in English.

we prayed for were healed. I admit there are no simplistic and clear answers to this puzzle.

This book is not a theology of healing, for that you should see Ken's books – *Healing in the Old Testament* and *Healing in the New Testament* – both available from Vision Publishing. It is instead an attempt to uncover some of the mystery that surrounds the healings God graciously gives to his people. It is also an affirmation of the many times the Lord has moved and folk have been healed through his mighty power. The testimonies in this book range in time from sixty years ago to just a few weeks before I wrote these words. Each one has been chosen to show God's goodness and his sovereignty. In Psalm 103 David rejoiced in the healing, delivering power of God.

Praise the Lord, O my soul; all my innermost being, praise his holy name. Praise the Lord, O my soul, and forget not all his benefits – who forgives all your sins and heals all your diseases, who redeems your life from the pit and crowns you with love and compassion, who satisfies your desires with good things so that your youth is renewed like the eagle's. (Ps 103:1-5)

These verses indicate healing on three levels, a cleansing from sin, a healing from bodily disease and a final redemption from eternal death.

We are promised healing, it is God's desire for healing to be available to his people (1 Pe 2:24), yet some do not receive the healing they claim. Healing miracles seem to happen without any definite pattern.

During our years in local church ministry we observed the Holy Spirit moving in waves of healing and then withdrawing for a time to come yet again in another wave of healing and deliverance. God has his reasons, we cannot know them, nor why he moves as he does in different places at different times.

Not everyone we prayed for was healed, but we felt this did not mean we should stop praying for the sick! We knew that if we stopped praying then no one would be healed through the prayer of faith. Because of this decision we observed many wonderful answers to prayer for which we praise God.

Those interested in learning about divine healing are taught that as we take God at his Word, through faith, seeking a point of contact and a precise moment in time when God will move, and then release our faith by doing what we could not do before, we will be rewarded by a healing. While victory over sickness does not always come so simply, there are many times when it does.

One of the times God healed me followed this set pattern.

After bathing at the local swimming pool at the Launceston Gorge I returned home in our car while a cool wind blew on my left shoulder. Next day I was immobilized with severe fibrositis and for one week was unable to dress as the pain was too great. I could not do any housework as I suffered day and night, becoming more debilitated as the week progressed. Sunday came and I determined I would attend the communion service for prayer. I was prayed for and then questioned myself, *"What is the first thing I would do if I was healed?"*

Straight away the answer came to me, *"I would go home and do the work I have been unable to do all week."* I returned home to clean and tidy my home and do all the work I had neglected while I was in pain. I was totally healed from then on.

Healing has come to many by this method. First the anointing with oil and then prayer as taught in the New Testament (Ja 5:14-16), followed by a release of faith and a stepping out to do what could not be done before.

But why is not everyone healed who follows this pattern?

Some earnest seekers, even after they feel they have done all that is required of them, do not receive the healing for which they long.

Let me make clear at the outset that this is not a book about "faith healing". This is different from divine healing and can come from many sources.

"Faith healing" can cause much disappointment and bewilderment in Christian circles. People who are taught wrongly can become disillusioned and sometimes even fall away from their Christian faith because they are promised more than is sensible or correct.

Hudson Taylor's Experience

Hudson Taylor in one of his letters home describes how

God showed him the correct way to view the healing message. While going through a time of great peril at sea and expecting any moment to be ship-wrecked he learned the lesson that God requires us first of all to do everything we can for ourselves and then ask Jesus to bless and heal as only he can:

> One thing was a great trouble to me that night. I was a very young believer, and had not sufficient faith in God to see him in and through the use of means. I had felt it a duty to comply with the earnest wish of my mother, and for her sake, to procure a swimming belt. But in my own soul I felt as if I could not simply trust in God while I had it, and my heart had no rest until on that night, after all hope of being saved was gone, I had given it away. Then I had perfect peace, and strange to say put several light things together, likely to float at the time we struck, without any thought of inconsistency!
>
> After the storm was over, the question was settled for me through the prayerful study of the Scriptures. God gave me then to see my mistake; probably to deliver me from a great deal of trouble on similar questions. It is a mistake that is very common in these days, when erroneous teaching on "faith" healing does much harm, misleading some as to the purposes of God, shaking the faith of others and distressing the minds of many. When in medical or surgical charge of any case, I have never thought of neglecting to ask God's blessing in the use of appropriate means, nor yet of omitting to give thanks for answered prayer and restored

health. It would now appear to me as presumptuous and wrong to neglect the use of those measures which he himself has put within our reach, as to neglect to take daily food, and suppose that life and health might be maintained by prayer alone.[3]

In Taylor's biography it is related that early in his marriage, through prayer, he did experience healing for his wife when she was at death's door, but in later years many of his missionaries died of various diseases because of their sojourn in China. Great are the mysteries in the heart of God! Their sacrifice was not in vain as the present Christian Church in China is the result of the many sacrifices made by those early missionaries from all denominations.

"Faith healing" as mentioned by Hudson Taylor is different from the "divine healing" we are concerned about in this book. Faith healing puts the burden on the individuals concerned, as if by thinking and praying hard enough they can force God to answer their prayer for healing. Divine healing on the other hand puts the burden on God and his promise in scripture, there should be no strain, just simple trust in the goodness of God.

Steps to Claiming the Promises

The steps we should take to claim any promise of God to the fulfilment of his promise are clear. Be it for healing, guidance or any other of his great promises.

---

3 Dr. & Mrs Howard Taylor, <u>Biography of James Hudson Taylor</u>, Hodder and Stoughton, 1965. pg. 86-87.

- We must receive a revelation, a "rhema" word, a "now" word, from the Lord for the promise we are claiming for ourselves.[4]

- There must be a commitment to the promise. (Pr 3:5-6)

- There must come a researching of the promise, (Ps 119 169-170) and a willingness to allow God to search our heart. (Ps 139:23-24)

- Then prayer without ceasing should be lifted to the Lord – this kind of prayer concerns a person's heart attitude being directed toward God at all times. (1 Th 5:17)

- Then we must be prepared for a testing of the promise – there will come a temptation to give up. Jesus suffered being tempted and we also must expect it and answer with the Word as he did. (Lu 4:1-13)

---

[4] W. E. Vine, Expository Dictionary of NT Words, Lowe and Brydon (printers) Ltd. London 1940. pg. 230. "The significance of a "rhema" word (as distinct from "logos") is exemplified in the injunction to take *"the sword of the Spirit which is the word of God"* In Ep 6:17 the reference is not to the whole Bible as such but to the individual scripture which the Spirit brings to our remembrance for use in time of need, a prerequisite being the regular storing of the mind with Scripture."

From my own experience a "rhema" (a now word) can be a scripture that is made revelation to us or it may also be a word of knowledge that comes to us from another Christian. Secondly it could come from something we read in a book or magazine that witnesses to our spirit as being a message to us from the Holy Spirit. In whatever way the "rhema" word comes to us the revelation of it brings a sure and certain faith to our spirit that nothing can destroy, faith rises and the work is accomplished.

- The final fulfilment of the promise will be ours if we remain faithful. (2 Co 1:20)
- Praise and worship then wells up in our hearts to the God of the promise for his answer to our prayers. (Ps 150:2; Acts 3:1-10)

Many of the healing testimonies in this book follow this pattern, yet in the mystery of God not all who receive prayer are able, for one reason or another, to grasp the full measure of the promise of healing. Only the Lord knows the answer to this mystery! One day all will be made clear to us and we must be patient until that time comes. The irony is, of course, that when we see him we will no longer care about the mystery, we will just be so filled with joy in his presence!

Let us explore the ministry of Jesus to see if we can understand why he had such complete success in bringing healing to sufferers during the years of his incarnation.

CHAPTER THREE

THE MINISTRY OF JESUS

Jesus was anointed, set apart, commissioned by God to preach good news to the poor, to bind up the broken hearted, to proclaim freedom for the captives, release from darkness for the prisoners, to comfort all those who mourn, and provide for those who grieve. (Is. 61: 1-3) His task was encapsulated in Acts 10:38 and his ministry proven by the healings that he accomplished throughout his ministry

God anointed Jesus of Nazareth with the Holy Spirit and power, and... he went around doing good and healing all who were under the power of the devil, because God was with him...When evening came, many who were demon possessed were brought to him, and he drove out the spirits with a word and healed all the sick. This was to fulfil what was spoken through the prophet Isaiah - He took up our infirmities and carried our diseases. (Mt 8:16-17; Is 53:4 see also Mark 1:32-34)

In Matthew 8:16 we are told Jesus healed all the sick. There was no one in whom Jesus discerned faith to be healed that went away disappointed. Even in Nazareth he found a few sick people who had faith for healing. (Mk 6:5) The healings Jesus performed were proof of his role as redeemer, solid proof that the kingdom of God had come into the world.

Characteristics of Jesus

There are some interesting facts we can learn about the life and ministry of Jesus to help us in our understanding of the healing ministry.

1. He was anointed for the task. As we have seen in many prophecies concerning his first coming he was to be set apart for the task of healing, it was part of the proof of his Sonship. (Is 61:1-2) His ministry of healing and signs and wonders was a certain proof of who he was. (Acts 2:22-24)

2. Jesus had the Holy Spirit without measure. (Jn 3:34)

3. Jesus had perfect discernment. He knew what was in the heart of each man and woman, nothing was hidden from him. (Jn 2:24-25)

4. Jesus was careful to say only those things that his Father told him to say and to do only those things God indicated he should do. (Jn 12:49; 14:10)

5. Jesus radiated a mixture of love, compassion, and authority received from his Father. Therefore the common people loved and trusted him and heard him gladly. (Mt 9:35-36; 14:14)

Jesus is the only one for whom all of these things were true during his earthly ministry. We do not have the Holy Spirit without measure, nor perfect discernment of the hearts of others. We can, however, be obedient to the Father as far as we are able; we can show the love of God and the compassion of the Holy Spirit to the sick and suffering, and Christ himself has passed on to us the authority given to him by his Father. (Mt 28:18)

Jesus first gave authority to his twelve disciples —

He called his twelve disciples to him and gave them authority to drive out evil spirits and to heal every disease and sickness. (Mt 10:1)

Then he sent out seventy-two others and to them he said,

I saw Satan fall like lightning from heaven. I have given you authority to trample on snakes and scorpions and to overcome all the power of the enemy; nothing will harm you. (Lu 10:18)

The last words Jesus spoke to his followers before his final ascension into heaven are recorded in Acts 1:8-9.

But you will receive power when the Holy Spirit comes on you; and you will be my witnesses in Jerusalem, and in all Judea and Samaria, and to the uttermost parts of the earth. After he said this, he was taken up before their very eyes, and a cloud hid him out of their sight.

There is no doubt, considering the subsequent actions of the apostles and other disciples and the many miraculous healings which took place, that Jesus wanted his healing authority to continue through his disciples. They were to go out into the world and preach the gospel, the good news from God, and to set free those who were bound in any way.

Faith seems to be the strong and definite precursor to healing as was made clear when Jesus returned to his home town.

He could not do any mighty miracles there, except lay his

hands on a few sick people and heal them. And he was amazed at their lack of faith. (Mk 6:5-6)

A Variety of Method

Jesus used a variety of ways in his healing ministry and this in itself is a mystery.

- He touched people. (Mt 8:14-15; Mk 1:41)
- He spoke a word. (Mt 8:16)
- He rebuked Satan. (Mk 1:21-28)
- He allowed people to touch him. (Lu 6:19)
- He prayed twice. (Mk 8:22-26)
- He used clay and spittle. (Jn 9:1-7)
- He healed from a distance by a word. (Jn 46-54)
- He put derisive, unbelieving people out of a room before praying. (Mk 5:35-43)
- He forgave sin as well as bringing healing. (Mk 2:1-12)
- He spat and touched the tongue of a deaf and dumb man. (Mk 7:31-37)

What can we learn from these methods of Jesus?

Jesus' ministry indicates we should not pray for everyone in the same way, using a set formula. We should not expect God to heal in the same way each time. God proves to us in many ways that he cannot be put into neat compartments, he is Sovereign, so we should pray and ask God for directions before we pray specifically for a person's healing.

Do we need any special anointing to heal the sick?

Some are given a special gift (1 Co 12:1-11), but even without this gift all Christians can lay hands on the sick when they are asked. Every saint has the potential to pray for those who need healing. Through the cross, and the Baptism in the Holy Spirit, God has already accomplished all that is needed for the sick to be healed through our prayers. It is up to us to be obedient to his desire for us to go into the world and preach the good news of salvation, for spirit, soul and body. (Mk 16:15-18)

We should go forward in his strength and do what he has asked us to do. He will guide and direct us into the path we need to follow as we put our full trust in him.

John G. Lake, a mighty healing evangelist of the early twentieth century, was given wonderful gifts of faith, healing and miracles so that it seems almost all he prayed for were healed. However, one time when he was demonstrating the gift of healing he prayed for five people in the company of many witnesses. Three of the people he prayed for were healed instantly, one was healed after a few days, and the fifth one died. Another mystery! [5]

Over fifty years of ministry with my husband I have learned several things about healing.

1. Some who pray for the sick emphasise the power of God others put more weight on showing love and compassion. We should seek a balanced approach. We must first claim

---

[5] Kenneth Copeland (Ed.), John G. Lake – His Life, His Sermons, His Boldness of Faith; Kenneth Copeland Publications, Fort Worth, Texas. 1994. pg. 269.

the authority (Lu 9:1-2; 10:18-19) promised us in scripture and then pray for the compassion to use this authority wisely.

2. If healing does not come immediately there could be a reason. It may not be God's time to heal a given person, or there are some things he wants to show that person first before healing takes place. Perhaps it is God's intention to bring healing through another person's prayers at a different time and place. Therefore we should not demand God to heal a particular person at a definite time; we should not expect God to heal when and where we think he should.

Do not feel a failure if a person is not healed through your prayers, leave them in God's hands, he is the only one who knows all things. He may bring them healing through some other means.

> Not one moment's pain is given you to bear that could have been dispensed with. Each has been the subject of divine consideration before permitted to come, and each will be removed directly its needed mission is fulfilled. (*F. B. Meyer*)[6]

3. Sometimes faith for healing can be blocked by the intense emotions of the next of kin.

4. It is possible that sometimes the Lord delays a healing (Mk 5:35) to bring greater glory to his name. We should not stop praying for healing!

---

[6] F. B. Meyer, The Way Into the Holiest, Marshall, Morgan and Scott, London. 1950. pg. 151.

In one instance the four reasons above were worked out clearly in my own life.

Healed of Endometriosis

Thirty years ago I went through a period of severe pain. This would come upon me suddenly and would cause me so much stabbing agony I would be immobilised for several hours. My husband would pray for me, the agony would recede for a space, and I would be able to resume the duties of a busy wife and mother of four. This went on for some months. In between the bouts of pain I would feel quite normal. Because of this it was several months before I finally went to a specialist to find out the cause. He examined me and confirmed I had endometriosis.

His decision was, *"When the pain becomes too great I will operate and perform a hysterectomy as there is no cure for this complaint!"*

A few weeks later I was in our Sunday communion service and, Ken being away in ministry elsewhere, our local pastor indicated he felt God's power to heal was present in a special way that day. If there were any sick in the congregation they were to come forward and they would be healed. Immediately I felt an overwhelming faith course through me, speeding like an arrow to my heart, this word was true! I knew that if I went forward I would be healed and from that day to this I have had no more pain and I have not had to have a hysterectomy.

Thinking over this healing I came to several conclusions.

1. I am convinced that my husband's deep emotion, caused by watching my suffering, blocked his faith.

2. Had God healed me the first time my husband prayed I would not have known the seriousness of my complaint or of the need for an operation. Because of the delay the Lord received more glory by my deliverance.

3. Even though I was not healed when my husband prayed for me God was preparing for my eventual healing in the future.

4. God used someone else's prayers. The pastor encouraged the people to come forward and join in praying for the sick that day and Stanlyn Swain, a teenager from the church, was impressed to pray for me.

Last of all I was able to bring faith for healing to others, for there is a sequel to this story, another amazing instance of the grace of God.

The Sequel

Twelve years went by and I was giving the testimony of my healing to a group of ladies in Melbourne, telling them of God's healing mercy given so graciously to me. After the meeting concluded a lady approached me on behalf of her daughter-in-law, who also had endometriosis, to ask if I would write to her and outline my testimony of how the Lord had healed me. This I did, and several months later I received this letter sent on the 12th January 1993.

The Wonder and the Mystery of Divine Healing
Alison Chant

Dear Alison,

I hardly know where to start this letter, but firstly I wish to thank you so much for writing to me late last year after my mother-in- law spoke with you – thank you for praying for me whilst I was so dreadfully ill; this touched me greatly as even though we don't know each other, your having had endometriosis and being healed encouraged me more than anyone could fathom. I was booked for surgery 3rd December, for a procedure, including removal of the left ovary and left fallopian tube, as these were badly diseased by the endometriosis. But, 8 days prior to the surgery date, the Lord performed his wonderful miracle of healing – I said to my husband that evening, "*I feel normal!*"

I knew the endometriosis had been dealt with then and there, and spoke this to very many of my friends and family. I did proceed with surgery on 3rd December as I was in great pain from many bowel adhesions, but was free of the pain of the endometriosis, of which I had become so used. The bowel adhesions were lasered, and after surgery an assistant surgeon walked to my husband, smiling, and told him all the surgeons could find was, "shrivelled up evidence of dead endometriosis cells!" Praise God, these words had been our <u>specific</u> prayer. The surgeons, general practioners, and others in the medical teams are differing in their acceptance of a miracle healing – some believe this, others are sceptical, but we know, accept, believe and testify to everyone of this wonderful gift from our precious Saviour.

Thank you again for your faithfulness, your encouragement and your testimony.

Your sister in Christ, Liz Stevenson

Ken's Healing

Another instance of healing delayed occurred during our ten years in the USA. My husband Ken had some agonising attacks of pain over several months and we prayed for him as a family without result. His doctor was convinced he had a diseased gall bladder, some form of cancer, or an aneurism. After making an appointment for an x-ray Ken asked for specific prayer. He was prayed for by Pastor Alan Langstaff, of Vision Ministries, and a Lutheran pastor, Rev. Rod Lensch. They agreed together with Ken for a complete healing.

Meanwhile I had been filled with fear as I had visions of what could be the outcome of my husband's sickness. The day before the x-ray was to be taken I was awoken by the Lord in the early hours of the morning with these words going through my mind, *"With long life will I satisfy him and show him my salvation"* (Psalm 91:16).

Immediately faith flowed into my spirit and I knew all would be well. When Ken went for the x-ray the doctor was amazed to find nothing wrong. He had been so sure that there was a serious problem. He asked for another x-ray but still the result was negative. There was great rejoicing in our home that day!

CHAPTER FOUR

DO YOU WANT TO GET WELL?

Now there is in Jerusalem near the Sheep Gate a pool, which in Aramaic is called Bethesda and which is surrounded by five covered colonnades. Here a great number of disabled people used to lie – the blind, the lame, the paralysed. One who was there had been an invalid for thirty eight years. When Jesus saw him lying there and learned that he had been in this condition for a long time, he asked him, "Do you want to get well?"

"Sir", the invalid replied, "I have no one to help me into the pool when the water is stirred. While I am trying to get in, someone else goes down ahead of me."

Then Jesus said to him, "Get up! Pick up your mat and walk". At once the man was cured; he picked up his mat and walked. (Jn 5:1-9)

The Man at the Pool of Bethesda

Why did Jesus heal only one person in that great throng of needy people?

There are four lessons we can draw from this story.

<u>**First,**</u> <u>the man was waiting in faith</u>. We cannot know for sure but it appears probable that Jesus perceived that only this one man had the faith to be healed and he had been waiting patiently for thirty eight years!

Lesson one. No one should despair of gaining healing from God. We should never cease to pray and believe, by building our faith on God's word, and by hearing testimonies, from others who have been healed, to strengthen our faith.

Second, he was willing to be healed. Jesus said, *"Do you want to get well?"* This was a strange question. The man was at the pool, he had placed himself in a position to be healed, he was doing all he could for himself. But not everyone who is sick wants to be healed! Some enjoy the sympathy and help they get from others while they are ill, they would rather not have to work for a living. This man, however, had a genuine desire to be whole and to be able to work. He did not want to beg any longer for his daily food.

Lesson two. If we are sick we need to be sure we want to get well and we should prepare ourselves for God to move in our life. How can we do this? First, by doing all we know to do for ourselves. In a spiritual sense we should let nothing stand between us and God, no sin; (Is 59:1-2) no un-forgiveness; (Mk 11:25) no bitterness, (He 12:14-15) or anything else contrary to the will of God for our life. (Ro 12:1-2) We should make sure to perform any acts of repentance or restoration needed to make things right with our fellow man.

Second, in a physical sense we should not despise the help we can get from obeying health and exercise principles or the advice we can receive from our health professional.

Third, the man began to walk in obedience. Immediately Jesus spoke the crippled man was willing and eager to rise up, pick up his bed and walk, even though he knew it was the Sabbath day and he could be arrested for carrying his bed roll on the Sabbath! His faith was an active faith that resulted in him doing something he couldn't do before.

Lesson three. We need to be obedient to all of God's revealed will. We need to read his Word, meditate on it, and note anything we should be doing, or that we should not be doing in our life.

Anything and everything that needs to be dealt with should be attended to through the blood of Jesus and the power of the cross. God is omni-present and well able to speak to each one of us about even the smallest detail of our life. If we prepare ourselves and seek him diligently then through his Word and through the Holy Spirit he will reveal spiritual truth to us. (Jn 16:13-15) We should then obey those things the Holy Spirit prompts us to do, and ask God to touch and heal areas in our life which need to change.

When we have made sure of all these things we should seek prayer for healing and then activate our faith to begin to do what we could not do before

Fourth, he was warned by Jesus. The words of Jesus were plain and clear, *"See, you are well again. Stop sinning or something worse may happen to you!"* (Jn 5:14b) We aren't told why the man became sick, though from what Jesus said he had evidently committed a sin which brought on the sickness.

Lesson four. Perhaps we have committed no gross sin but many of us neglect our health, and do not take sufficient exercise. If our way of life caused the sickness in the first place and we do not change then the sickness could return again.

Another consideration to ponder from this story is that the rest of the people were so intently watching the water they missed seeing Jesus. Perhaps the man in our story was the only one who was watching for him!

This is something we who live in the more affluent nations should note. We have so many ways of seeking healing and dealing with pain that we lack the single minded purpose needed to seek Jesus for healing. A Christian person in a poorer country without easy access to doctors and hospitals must rely greatly on Jesus and his healing power. Their desperation of faith is perhaps the reason why we see God working in healing power so much more in their world than we do in rich countries like our own.

More Mysteries

Sometimes a special manifestation is given to someone for a season and then is taken away again. This happened to a friend of mine, Pastor Helen Beard, in Mildura, Victoria. Helen for a season was able to tell people for whom she was praying what vitamins or minerals were needed in their diet. To one she might say, *"You need vitamins* (such as) *A & E"*; to another, *"You are missing a certain mineral* (such as) *iron or zinc."*

If the persons seeking healing then took these ingredients they would recover from the illness that afflicted them. Helen does not know why God gave her this gift, or why he gave it only for a season.

John G. Lake, already mentioned, was also given a special gift for a limited time. This gift enabled him to go into a hospital, lay hands on a person, and immediately tell what was wrong with the patient. He did this for doctors who called him in to their hospital whenever they were baffled by a patient's symptoms. This gift too, was only given for a period. Lake did not know why it was given or why it was removed. These phenomena must remain a mystery that only God understands. They are a sign and a wonder! [7]

Why are some persons healed instantly and some not for days, weeks, months or even years?

One answer could be that an instant healing is an apparent miracle, but actually an acceleration of the natural healing of our body by the power of God. A slower healing could be God blessing by helping our body heal at the normal pace. In his wisdom God has designed our body to heal itself and he has also given different natural remedies for us to use in various herbs and other plants. We must do for ourselves what we can and ask God's blessing on our efforts, for all healing ultimately comes from him.

If we seek God earnestly to understand the lessons of faith we need to learn, then over time our faith can grow and develop to the point we are able to believe for greater and greater manifestations of the healing power of God.

---

[7] Gordon Lindsay (Ed.), The New John G. Lake Sermons, Gordon Lindsay Publications, Christ For The Nations, 1971. pg. 17.

Why are unbelievers sometimes healed, before they have acknowledged Jesus as Lord and Saviour, in contrast with saints who have been saved for years and yet are not healed?

In our experience God in his mercy has performed some miraculous healings in people who are not born again, though usually they do accept Christ as Saviour subsequent to their healing.

Does God then expect more from a Christian of many years standing than he does from a non-believer?

From everyone who has been given much, much will be demanded; and from the one who has been entrusted with much, much more will be asked. (Lu 12:48b)

Jesus, in this whole passage (Lu 12:42-48) refers to his Second Coming, but the principle is clear; if we know more then more is expected in the way of faith in the healing promise.

Can we say to Christians they are not healed because of their lack of faith?

"*No!*" An individual should never be accused of lack of faith, nor made to feel guilty because he/she is not healed. Blame rather the lack of faith and expectation in the church.

However, it is possible for the Christian that God wants to teach us some things before he heals us. Certainly his expectations of us will be higher than his expectation from an unbeliever who knows nothing of the Word of God or of faith.

Why does God work mightily in a new area where his power has not been seen, and not so mightily in the church?

Many times we have heard of God manifesting his power in a new area where his Word has never been preached before in faith. On the other hand, in the church he expects Christians to know the Word and walk in health. Many times the Holy Spirit is asked to bring healing in the church where the saints are already aware of their pathway to healing (Ja 5:14) when he should rather be asked to bring healing out in the market place to those beyond the confines of the church. (Mk 16:15)

Missionaries Amazed

I remember years ago hearing the story of a group of Lutheran missionaries who were expelled from Ethiopia. They left their converts with a Bible and bade them keep strong in the Lord.

Many years later they were allowed to return to the mission and they found the Ethiopians were being baptised in the Holy Spirit as on the day of Pentecost and seeing miracles of healing! The missionaries were amazed, and said to the people, *"Why is this so."*

The Christians replied, *"We found these things in the Bible and we claimed them for ourselves."*

I believe that God shows his power in these circumstances because he is watching to see that his Word is fulfilled (Je 1:12). God will always stand behind his Word and make sure that his power is manifest in an area where people have never before known he has the power to heal and deliver.

Taking all of these mysteries into account we must agree however that God is in control of our final destiny, and freely acknowledge that sometimes he does allow Christians to die while they are still young. This could happen in times of war; persecution; periods of famine, disastrous earthquakes and tidal waves as well as just part of the inscrutable purposes of God. (1 Co 13:12)

Boundaries to Healing

There are five other limitations of which we should be aware. [8]

> 1. The gifts of healing are not intended to restore youth to old age, though it does happen that people do feel younger and more alert and energetic if they are living in harmony with God's will for them. We see this in Moses (De 34:7) and in Caleb. (Js 14:10-11)
>
> 2. Some people have broken the laws of health over a period of years, and even now are still doing the same, yet they expect a miracle of healing to atone for all this.
>
> 3. Healing does not ordinarily restore missing organs, although this has been known to happen.

---

[8] Gordon Lindsay, Bible Days Are Here Again; Published by Gordon Lindsay; 1949; pg. 181-184)

During the ministry of Jesus a possible miracle of restoration occurred. (Jn 9:6; Lu 22:50-51)

4. <u>Healing is not to take the place of the natural processes of life</u>. If a person of twenty years of age who had a retarded brain was healed then it would take him twenty years to mature to the level of another twenty- year- old. However if demon possession was the reason a person appeared to be retarded then it might be possible for instant healing to occur.

5. <u>There are some human infirmities which it seems impossible to avoid</u>. Divine healing seems to retard, but does not altogether arrest the processes of age. For instance Elisha was bald. (2 Kings 2:23)

Lessons to Be Learned

Lesson One: We cannot live forever in this world though we are promised three score years and ten, or eighty if we have the strength (Ps 90:10; Pr 3:1-2). After that there must come a time for us all to go and be with the Lord. There came such a time for Elisha, even though he had such a miraculous ministry throughout his life. We read in Second Kings 13:14, *"Now Elisha was suffering from the illness from which he died..."*

We are promised in Psalm 103:5 that, *"your youth is renewed like the eagle's!"* It is fascinating to learn how eagles go through the stages of renewal. This does not come about quickly or easily.

High in the mountains, the eagle proceeds to go through a remarkable process of rejuvenation.

Firstly it starts to pluck at some of its wing feathers. One by one the faulty feathers are "cast out"...While awaiting the regrowth of its flight feathers, the eagle does something about a dull beak – perhaps blunted by rocks or the growth of calcium build up. The beak is an all important weapon and must be kept lethally sharp. Like a soldier preparing his sword for battle, the calcifications are painstakingly ground away by the slow but steady action of the beak against the rock. Likewise the talons too may be sharpened or removed altogether. Relentlessly the beak and talons are honed back to lethal sharpness, ready for the world...Eventually after many days of preening, plucking, honing, grinding and washing, the eagle is ready to return to the outside world. It spreads its huge wings and alights from the mountain peaks, a new bird. Its youth has been renewed.[9]

How wonderful that our Father has promised us renewal as we put our trust in him, both in our body and also in our spirit – we will run and not grow weary, we will walk and not faint because our hope is in him. (Is 40:30-31)

Lesson Two: We cannot expect God to heal us when we break the laws of health. We should first do what we can for ourselves before we ask God for a miracle. We should also treasure the healing miracle God does for us and not throw it away through disobedience.

---

[9] Col Stringer, <u>All About Eagles</u>, Col Stringer Ministries, Queensland, Australia.

One tragedy we witnessed was of an alcoholic whose favourite drink was pineapple juice laced with methylated spirits. God healed him mightily through prayer and for three months he was free of his disease. Unfortunately he thought he could continue to drink lightly and, even though we warned him not to go back to drinking any alcohol at all, he thought he knew better. Inevitably he returned to his former way of life and though he sought healing again God did not answer his prayers. God is not prodigal of his miracles!

We should each do all we can to bring glory to God, through prolonging our life and health so as to continue in ministry as long as the Lord requires.

Lesson Three: If a missing organ is restored then it would be more accurately termed a miracle rather than a healing.

Lesson Four: For those suffering mental illness God and prayer are very efficacious. During the '60's some of the Bible students from the Crusade Bible College, Adelaide, where my husband lectured, began meetings at the Parkside Mental Institution with the permission of the head doctor. They incorporated the singing of choruses and hymns; spoke to the people about the forgiveness of God and prayed for those who requested prayer. Before very long a significant number of patients were ready to go home, well and strong and able to take up their lives once more.

Lesson Five: We all need to be careful not to work too hard. One infirmity Christ shared with his disciples was human weariness. He often took his disciples apart to rest. (Mt 9:35-38; Mk 6:31b) So we also need to take time for rest and recreation to restore our energy levels. And we must accept the normal process of ageing (cp. Ec 12:1-5).

CHAPTER FIVE

HINDRANCES TO HEALING

Why are some Christian people sick and some not healed?

One reason may be because they have not discerned the Lord's body as they should:

For I received from the Lord what I also passed on to you: The Lord Jesus on the night he was betrayed, took bread, and when he had given thanks, he broke it and said, "This is my body, which is for you; do this in remembrance of me." In the same way, after supper he took the cup, saying, "This cup is the new covenant in my blood; do this, whenever you drink it, in remembrance of me." For whenever you eat this bread and drink this cup, you proclaim the Lord's death until he comes. Therefore, whoever eats the bread or drinks the cup in an unworthy manner will be guilty of sinning against the body and blood of the Lord. A man ought to examine himself before he eats of the bread and drinks of the cup. For anyone who eats and drinks without recognising the body of the Lord eats and drinks judgment on himself. That is why many among you are weak and sick, and a number have fallen asleep. But if we judged ourselves we would not come under judgment. (1 Co 11:23-31)

Communion is Important

1. The communion table is where Christians should first begin to prepare themselves for healing. As Christians we need to know the importance of the communion of the saints. We are told we must discern the Lord's body, to see it clearly with our mind or intellect. This is not properly understood by some Christians.

What does it mean?

We must understand that the bread and the cup signify that we are remembering the New Covenant that Jesus made for us. (Lu 22:14-20) Each time we take the sacraments we must be aware of the tremendous sacrifice of Jesus our Saviour, we must not take these elements lightly, but soberly, examining ourselves to see if there is any sin in our life, and confessing our need for the Saviour. As we take the bread and the cup we are proving we believe the words of Jesus:

"I tell you the truth, unless you eat the flesh of the Son of man and drink his blood, you have no life in you. Whoever eats my flesh and drinks my blood has eternal life, and I will raise him up at the last day. For my flesh is real food and my blood is real drink. Whoever eats my flesh and drinks my blood remains in me and I in him." (Jn 6: 53-56)

Understanding, and obeying, the law of our relationship with Jesus brings health, happiness and well-being. The greatest miracle concerning the healing message surely is one of continued health with no sickness at all coming into our life.

With the cup we celebrate the forgiveness of our sins given to us by Jesus our Saviour, and this in itself earns us a mental, emotional, and spiritual health that is not available to those outside of Christ. (1 Jn 1:8-9) With the bread, we celebrate the healing power of Jesus and reach out for physical healing when we need it. (Is 53:5; Jn 6:35)

I am convinced that as we take the bread, and the cup, Sunday by Sunday, and as we place our life in the hands of the Lord, he moves to heal us and to keep us well. For this reason it is sad to see so many congregations these days taking communion on an irregular basis, some once a month, some once a year. No wonder power has gone out of the church!

> God's healing can come in different ways. By a sovereign act, by signs and wonders to attract people to God, and by man's response of faith in God's covenant promise. (Alan Langstaff)[10]

The opposite of the healing virtue, available in communion, is also true. The Apostle Paul warns us, if we do not discern the Lord's body as we should then we can become sick and even die.

For anyone who eats and drinks without recognising the body of the Lord eats and drinks judgment on himself. That is why many among you are weak and sick, and a number of you have fallen asleep. (1 Co 11:29-30)

2. We must discern the Lord's body in the church. (1

---

[10] Alan Langstaff (Lecture) <u>The Healing Covenant</u>; Vision Bible College, Sydney, Australia 1978.

Co 12:26) Our brothers and sisters in Christ must be held in esteem. If we injure another member of the body of Christ, then we injure ourselves, for we also belong to that same body. A proper relationship with our fellow brothers and sisters brings health to our own bodies.

Salt is good, but if it loses its saltiness how can you make it salty again? Have salt in yourselves, and be at peace with each other. (Mk 9:50)

Salt is for preservation, to keep food from deteriorating, so in a sense it **stands for good health**. It **also indicates fellowship;** in eastern lands if you share your salt then you pledge not to injure your neighbour. A **peaceful life can also lead us toward health** and we are called to live in peace and to be grateful for our blessings. (Cl 3:15)

Proper relationships within the body of Christ bring health to it. As we live in peace with one another we strengthen the body and prepare it for the great works God has planned should be done. (Cl 3:12-15)

Weaker members of the body should be held up by the stronger, so those who are strong in faith for healing should help others who are weak in faith, and those who are strong in their stand against Satan, and all his works, should protect the weaker brethren from evil. (Ga 6:1-2; Ro 15:1-2)

3. **Then we must discern the Lord's body in the wider sphere of the world.** There is no room for lack of love toward other denominations, nor any room for dogmatism that can injure the body of Christ. We can show our love for the wider body by praying for missions,

and upholding missionaries, and those who are being persecuted for their belief in Christ.

More Hindrances

1. Healing can also be prevented by forgetting that our bodies are the temples of the Holy Spirit. (1 Co 6:15-19) Christians can abuse their bodies by taking insufficient rest, by smoking, or eating more than is good for them, or drinking alcohol to excess. In the same way

that we keep our bodies from sin we should avoid those things which will bring us into weakness or sickness of any kind.

We should not forget that we are subject to physical laws and therefore should not work too hard, even if it is God's work we are doing!

Sometimes men and women of God who have been used in healing have become sick themselves through overwork, or not taking proper care of their health. Kathryn Kuhlman developed an enlarged heart and finally had to have a heart operation, yet she had spectacular results in the healing ministry.[11]

2. Healing can be hindered if we do not take time to prepare our hearts. As Christians we must make sure that the Word of God dwells in us richly; we must absorb it, and it must become revelation to us. (Cl 3:16) In this way God, and what he can do, becomes more real to us than our present circumstances, whether we are faced

---

[11] Kathryn Kuhlman (1903-1976), www. Christianheroes.com/ev/ev032.asp, pg.4.

with our own sickness or we have been asked to pray for someone else.

The Word of God must be absorbed, it must make the incredible journey from the head to the heart, from mere knowledge to spiritual revelation, and this takes time and meditation. The Word must become revelation knowledge to transform our thinking and believing. (Mk 9:23; Ep 1:15-23)

3. **Some people do not have sufficient faith**, they are not sure it is God's will to heal (Mt 17:14-20; Mk 1:41). This can be true of either the one being prayed for, the one praying for healing, or the other people in the meeting.

The climate of faith in the church needs to grow. Kathryn Kuhlman had more healings in her later ministry than she had when she first started preaching. Both her faith and the faith of her congregation grew over the years. We all need to grow in faith for mighty works to be done. (Ro 10:17)

Remember it is, *"these signs shall follow those who believe."* (Mk 16:17) The whole church needs to be strong in faith and not just the individual.

Jesus gave instruction to those wanting his healing and we also must teach people about healing to inspire their faith. **You get that for which you preach; if you want to see healings then you must preach healing**. Those of us who desire to see healings occur should rise up in righteous anger and preach against Satan, declaring freedom in Christ from sin, sickness and any weakness of the flesh.

It has been my experience that there is a great secret in feeling intense anger against Satan and all his works of sickness and bondage. It releases the power of God and our faith is set free to believe without any doubt that the devil was defeated at the cross for all time and eternity. (Lu 10:18)

We must face the fact of community unbelief as Jesus did in Nazareth (Mk 6:5) and preach against it. We live in a country that is no longer considered to be a Christian country. The kind of community faith that prevailed at the time of Jesus' ministry on earth is not possible when we are surrounded on all sides by unbelief. Preaching healing and seeing marvellous results will go a long way to raising the awareness of faith and to bringing deliverance from all kinds of bondages right here in our own land.

4. **Some attach a false value to suffering**, they believe it is redemptive. They feel their suffering is for a purpose. It is hard to pray for healing for people who believe in redemptive suffering. For healing to flow we must believe that it is God's will to heal.

The truth is that when Jesus was manifest in the flesh he came to show us his Father's heart. God is a healing God. It is his desire that all should be well.

5. **Some may have unconfessed sin in their life.** (Ja 5:13-16; Pr 28:13; Is 59:1-2) If we have sinned we must repent, and if we have injured someone then we should ask for forgiveness. An unforgiving spirit, and such things as bitterness, resentment of authority, and angry relationships can hinder healing. If we want healing we must make amends and restore fellowship. (Mt 18:21-35)

6. The desire for healing is not strong enough in some people. We must have a strong desire to be healed, *"Whatsoever things you desire when you pray."* (Mk 11:24 KJV) *"God is a rewarder of those who diligently seek him."* (He 11:6)

7. Some allow depression to overwhelm them and this dries up their faith for healing. Serving God with gladness and cheerfulness of heart (enthusiasm) was a condition for healing in the Old Testament. (De 28:47) *"A cheerful heart is good medicine but a crushed spirit dries up the bones."* (Pr 17:22)

8. There are those who stubbornly demand that God heal them without natural means and so refuse to see medicine as a way that God heals. (Sirach 38:12-14) Or, conversely, they lean totally on the arm of flesh, insisting on medical treatment only and do not also seek God's healing power; the mistake king Asa made long ago. (2 Ch 6:12) Paul had more sense and made use of doctor Luke's abilities. (Cl 4:14)

9. Perhaps the person seeking healing has been involved in the occult in some way, even if, as a child, they may have thought it was innocent play. (De 18:10) This needs to be repented of and renounced before prayers for healing are offered.

10. Healing may not come if there are bad relationships within the family for whom you are praying. When praying for a young child, if the parents of the child are unsaved, this may hinder the healing. Ensure the believing faith of a child's authority figure if that is possible.

11. Healing may not come if the person seeking healing does not act out his/her faith. Some of the healings recorded in this book show the person acting out their faith in a way that demonstrated their belief in the healing they had been promised. (2 Kg 5:1-14; Jn 9:7-11)

12. Sometimes the person is not steadfast in his/her faith. (Ja 1:5-8) If not healed immediately they cast away their faith. We should never give up expecting God to heal, in his own way and in his own time.

If all these issues are attended to and still the healing does not come; if the sickness prevails and a loved one goes to be with God, then we know at least in the resurrection that loved one will no longer be sick! God is Sovereign and we know that, *"Precious in the eyes of the Lord is the death of his saints."* (Ps 116:15) Jesus must at times long to welcome us face to face, to say, *"Well done good and faithful servant."* (Mt 25:21)

> We must trust God even if we do not always understand why he does not heal. It is better to die in faith than to live in unbelief. (Alan Langstaff)[12]

There is another mystery held in the heart of God, he may take a loved one because he sees something in their future that would bring some kind of evil into their life.

The righteous perish, and no one ponders it in his heart; devout men are taken away, and no one understands that the righteous are taken away to be spared from evil. (Is 57:1)

---

[12] Op. Cit.

Finding More Answers

Is it the will of God to heal all physical diseases and infirmites in his children or is it only some people he wills to heal?

We must find more answers in the words Jesus spoke and the work he did, because unless we can believe the healing message to be true then we set up a strong barrier to our faith!

Jesus made it clear while he was on the earth that all sickness and disease were against his will. Nearly the whole record of Christ's ministry to men and women is a record of constant warfare against the devil and all his works of sickness and disease.

If sickness and disease were a means of growing in grace, as some believe, then Jesus would have been opposing the will of the Father in his ministry! But this cannot be so, because Jesus said he only did the things his Father told him to do and he only said the things his Father told him to say. (Jn 5:36-40; 12:49-50)

Indeed he came to do the will of his Father as we saw in Acts 10:38.

Jesus called the sickness of the daughter of Abraham "*a bondage from Satan.*" (Luke 13:10-16) He never told anyone that it was good for them to suffer from a disease. Jesus healed constantly throughout the gospels; over and over we are told that he healed the sick (Mt 12:15; Mk 3:10; Lu 4: 40-41). The healing ministry of Christ was the ultimate proof that the kingdom of God had come.

Jesus proved that our salvation is complete, and our redemption concluded, by the healings he accomplished, and is still accomplishing today. He spent a large part of his ministry time of three and a half years in ministering to the sick.

These are some of the answers, but if we think we have all the answers then we shut ourselves off from gaining further knowledge. Healing is a mystery of God's love. What we can do in each individual case is:

First understand that our part is so to immerse ourselves in God's word and prayer that we are a fit vessel for him to use. Then, when asked to pray for someone we should turn to God in simple trust, accepting the fact that we do not have infinite knowledge of the person or of their sickness. We should then ask God to lead and guide us in the way he wants us to proceed and, last of all, we should pray with courage and boldness and then leave the results with God.

Concerning Chastening

In your struggle against sin, you have not resisted to the point of shedding your blood. And you have forgotten that word of encouragement that addresses you as sons: "My son, do not make light of the Lord's discipline, and do not lose heart when he rebukes you, because the Lord disciplines those he loves, and he punishes everyone he accepts as a son". <u>Endure hardship as discipline</u>; God is treating you as sons. (He 12:4-7a)

Discipline is not mentioned here as sickness, rather the type of discipline mentioned is hardship, such as the confiscation of goods, and persecution. (1 Pe 1:1-9)

Jesus himself learned obedience through the things that he suffered and he was never sick! (He 5:8) Our sufferings then should be similar to his for us to be <u>sharing</u> his sufferings. (1 Pe 4:1; 12-19)

However, Paul's instructions for communion do mention sickness as discipline:

That is why many among you are weak and sick, and a number of you have fallen asleep. But if we judged ourselves, we would not come under judgment. When we are judged by the Lord, we are being disciplined so that we will not be condemned with the world." (1 Co 11:30-32)

Sickness and disease came into this world through the disobedience of Adam and Eve, Because of the fall God allows sickness and disease in the same way that he allows sin. He has promised a way of escape from temptation to sin (1 Co 10:13) and he has made a way for us to be healed from sickness through the sufferings of Jesus on the cross (Is 53:5b). We do not have full victory over all sin in our lives as Christians and we won't until the resurrection! In the same way we do not have full victory over sickness in this life but we must, in both cases, continue to believe and reach out for each victory as it is needed.

Sickness is a terrible thing but because God can do all things he sometimes does bring good out of evil (Ro 8:28) which explains why some who are sick increase in holiness and goodness. On the other hand there are others who have become more irritable and shown less grace during times of sickness.

Can Sickness Return?

If we are healed but go on doing the same thing that caused the sickness in the first place then the sickness may return.

Satan attacks us when we first receive Christ as Saviour to get us to doubt. The same is true of our healing. We must answer Satan with Scripture as Jesus did in his temptation in the wilderness. (Lu 4:1-13) Remember, the promise will always be tested.

A retired minister of the Methodist church, Rev D. T. Reddin, who, during his lifetime, was a strong believer in divine healing, claimed there are three kinds of faith, historic faith, temporary faith and active faith. <u>Historic faith</u> covers our believing that Jesus died and rose again to bring us salvation. <u>Temporary faith</u> is the kind of faith a person may have for the period of time they are being prayed for. While the prayers are fresh in their mind they feel better but then, later their faith subsides and grows weak and they lose what they have gained. If the symptoms of their sickness return they may then throw away their faith and lose their healing. In chapter one of this book Mr Stan Shipp explains how this understanding helped him to claim his healing from angina pectoris, but only after he saw the difference between temporary faith and active faith. Once he saw that truth he realised he needed <u>active faith</u>, strong enough to claim his healing and to see it slowly but surely come to pass. He was then able to claim complete victory. [13]

---

[13] Rev. D. T. Reddin, art. <u>Revivalist.</u> September. 1968.

Those who pray for the sick should always be positive. A good pastor does not tell his people that they may lose their hold on Christ. Instead he teaches them the scriptures so they will not turn back from following the Saviour. In the same way an excellent teacher will not tell people they may lose their healing, rather he instructs them so they will keep it. (Ex 23:25-26; Pr 4:20-22Mk 5:21-43)

In this chapter we have covered some of the reasons why all are not able to claim their healing. However, when these things are dealt with one by one and our faith is strengthened then healing should come unless it is our time to go to be with the Lord.

There is yet another consideration.

What about the climate of faith in our churches? How strong is it?

Does the climate of faith need to be stronger before we can see more healings for the glory of God?

I believe it does. In the next chapter we see some ways of strengthening our faith.

CHAPTER SIX

A CLIMATE OF FAITH

What can we do to raise the climate of faith in our churches so that we can see God working more wonderfully than he has in past years?

First, it is always good to look back and see what God has done. There have always been people somewhere in this world since Old Testament days, who have believed God for healing and miracles.

One such story concerns the Scottish Covenanters. [14]

There was a young man, heir of Lord Ochiltree, who afterwards became Lord Castlestuart. He became ill, gradually wasted away and eventually died. Pastor Welch, who was responsible for the young man began to pray and would not stop. After twelve hours men came with a coffin but Pastor Welch would not give up and asked for more time. After twenty four hours they came again, then after thirty six hours, then forty eight hours, but he would not give up praying. There was still no sign of life!

Finally to please the pastor and convince him the young man was dead the men tied a string around

---

14 John Howie, Scots Worthies, Armoury Pub. www. pap.com.au; 2002.

his forehead and tightened it and then they pinched the young man's legs several times very roughly. There was no sign of life! Pastor Welch begged for just two more hours and he cried out to God in an agony of soul.

Then, at the end of those last two hours, the young man opened his eyes and cried out, *"O sir, I am well, but my head and my legs!"*

What a marvellous testimony of God's mercy and healing power. The young man was bruised by the rough handling he had received from those who were trying to prove he was dead. Fifty hours of heart rending prayers of intercession! Pastor Welch would not let God go until he blessed him by restoring his pupil to life.

How many times we may have missed a healing because we did not continue to pray until victory was granted. It seems to me that it is not until someone says something can't be done that God's power and glory can be shown in the best way.

In Switzerland Smith Wigglesworth prayed for a man blind from birth!

This blind man said he never had seen; he was born blind, but because of the Word preached in the afternoon he was not going home until he could see. If ever I have joy it is when I have a lot of people who will not be satisfied until they get all they have come for. With great joy I anointed him that day and laid hands on his eyes, and then immediately God opened his eyes. It was very strange how he acted. There were some electric lights. First he counted them; then he counted us. Oh the ecstatic pleasure that every moment was created in that man because of his sight! It made us feel like weeping and dancing and shouting. Then he pulled out his watch, and said that for years he had been feeling the watch for the time, by the raised figures, but now he could look at it and tell us the time. Then, looking as if he was awakened from some deep sleep, or some long, strange dream, he awakened to the fact that he had never seen the face of his father and mother, and he went to the door and rushed out. At night he was the first in the meeting. All the people knew him as a blind man, and I had to give him a long time to talk about his new sight.[15]

John Wesley, the founder of Methodism had a miraculous healing!

In his prime John Wesley contracted a severe attack of tuberculosis which caused him to compose an epitaph for his tomb.

Here Lieth the body
Of
John Wesley
A Brand plucked from the Burning
Who died of a Consumption in the fifty-first year
Of his Age,

---

[15] Roberts Liardon, Smith Wigglesworth – The Complete Collection of His Life Teachings, Albury Publishing, Tulsa, OK. USA. 1996. pg. 146.

> Not leaving, after his debts are paid,
> Ten pounds behind him:
> Praying:
> God be merciful to me, an Unprofitable Servant![16]

Praise God Wesley did not die, he was healed by the Lord at fifty-one years of age and lived on until 1791. He died on March 2nd in his eighty- eighth year. There was no need for the epitaph he had composed to be used!

Here is another quote from John Wesley's life, a testimony to his continued health and strength, this time from J. Boyd Nicholson.

> Wesley travelled 250,000 miles on horseback and averaged twenty miles a day for forty years. He preached 40,000 sermons and produced hundreds of books translated into ten languages.
>
> At eighty three years of age he was concerned that he could not write more than fifteen hours a day without hurting his eyes and was ashamed he could not preach more than twice a day. He noted in his journal that there was an increasing tendency to lie late in bed in the morning – until 5:30 am!

Second, we must continually feed upon the Word of God. It is the Holy Spirit that will produce faith in our heart. (Ro 10:17)

Third, we must commune with the Lord in prayer,

---

[16] Basil Miller, <u>John Wesley</u>, Bethany House Publishers, Minneapolis. MN. USA.

making sure that we confess any sin which may come between us and God, and pray without ceasing for his glory to be manifest. (Is 59:1-2; 1Th 5:16; 1Tim 2:1-4)

Fourth, we need to learn who we are in Christ and the authority he has given us to enter into a healing ministry. (1Co 12:1-11)

Having done all of these things we are still faced with the fact that not all who are prayed for are healed and we must ask ourselves:

Is it God's will to heal all sick people?

Experience says, *"No!"* because so many are not healed, but unless we believe the truth that it is God's will to heal everyone who comes to him in faith we maintain an impregnable barrier between us and God's healing power! Surely Jesus made it clear that he came to heal all manner of sickness and disease.

You may say what about someone like Joni Eareckson Tada? Joni is a lovely Christian lady who was paralysed from the neck down through a diving accident when in her teen years. She has since risen above her despair through her strong and rich faith in God and has become a well known Christian author. [17]

Remember the boundaries to healing? Joni would need a miracle rather than a simple healing. She would need a regrowth of nerves. This miracle has happened in the Chant family circle.

---

[17] www.powertochange.com/changed/jeareckson.html

Barry Chant's Healing

In 1960 my husband and I were boarding Ken's younger brother Barry while he attended Adelaide University. Barry contracted tonsillitis and was quite ill with a temperature, not eating for a few days. When Sunday came Barry, being a conscientious Christian, determined to attend the Cheltenham CRC church on his motorbike. I demurred as I felt he would be foolish to ride his bike after being so ill. We did not feel free to give permission, the reponsibility was too great, so Barry rang his father. Not realising that Barry had been fasting, he gave his permission. A circumstance which relieved my conscience but unfortunately proved deadly to Barry.

A Horrible Shock

We were half way through our own church service when the police arrived to let us know that Barry had apparently fainted on the bike and in swerving had hit a telegraph pole with his left shoulder. He was in the Adelaide hospital, not far from where we were in Sturt St. and we hastened to see him. He had a broken left upper arm and three of his top vertebrae were cracked.

The doctors did not realise at first that his spleen was also in fifteen pieces. It was only because one of the doctors pressed his unusual umbilical hernia and Barry cried out that the doctors recognised this life threatening danger. They quickly rushed him to the operating theatre to remove the spleen. The doctors said later that it was only because Barry had lived a clean life without smoking or drinking alcohol that he pulled through the ordeal of the operation.

His Recovery was Steady

His recovery was slow but steady and after some six weeks he was allowed to come home. Unfortunately because of his other more serious problems the doctors had not been able to attend to his upper left arm. When they finally checked his arm it had mended with the bone overlapping. This meant his left arm was now shorter than his right but even more serious was the fact the nerve of his upper arm had been torn and he now found that he could use his hand but could not lift his arm.

On his return home we watched helplessly at meal times as Barry had to lift his arm into position and then use his hand to cut his food. A terrible tragedy for this young man, only nineteen years of age, who had his whole life before him. He was engaged to a beautiful girl, Vanessa, and he had an arts degree to finish. He had plans for the future to become a pastor in a church which believed passionately in divine healing!

Determined to Believe

He determined to get his pastor, Dudley Cooper, to pray for him in the Cheltenham assembly on a certain Sunday during the church service, and then he set himself to believe for a miracle of answered prayer. During the day he had to wear a brace on his arm to go to classes at the University but in the evenings he decided to do some exercises to strengthen his arm. These had been prescribed by the physiotherapist in hope they would do some good. He would lay himself down on the carpet of the lounge room with a weight in his hand and attempt to lift his arm. Each time he tried to lift the weight he would breathe the name of Jesus in faith that the healing would come. He did this for around two months and then one day we heard a cry of triumph as he felt a flicker of life in his upper arm. From then on his arm gradually strengthened more each day until he could lift his arm in the air with no trouble at all.

Doctor Amazed

Shortly after this wonderful result he met his doctor on North Terrace, Adelaide. The doctor asked how Barry's arm was progressing. To his astonishment Barry raised his arm high. After congratulating him the doctor made the comment that if the nerve was going to regenerate it would take two to three months time after the regeneration for it to strengthen sufficiently to raise the arm. Looking back Barry realised that it was some three months from when his pastor had prayed for him until he felt the first tiny thrill of life flowing into his arm. The possibility is that the healing actually began when Dudley prayed but it took three months for the nerve to grow. We speculated, what if Barry had not attempted to lift that brick day after day in faith, would the Lord still have healed his arm? Certainly he would not have had the strength in it that he now had.

An Ongoing Miracle

The doctors warned Barry that, despite this wonderful occurrence, because of the removal of his spleen he would not in future have the energy of a normal man and he should temper his life accordingly. The Lord undertook here also as Barry's achievements over the years since his accident have far outstripped the work of a normal man. Having retired from building a flourishing Bible College which has spread to four states of Australia, he has now taken up the pastorate of a large church in downtown Sydney. At sixty-seven years of age he still plays tennis on a regular basis as well as keeping up a brisk walking schedule.

Here are some other wonderful healing miracles my husband and I have witnessed!

I first joined the CRC when I was fourteen years of age and I was baptised in the Holy Spirit in 1949. I remember the Sunday night Pastor Leo Harris preached on healing and Peter Perdikis was healed of tuberculosis. Peter had signed himself out of the Adelaide hospital to come to the Sunday night meeting. His doctors had warned him he had only a short time to live but he was determined to be prayed for and God honoured his faith. He was completely healed and later married.

During a healing campaign in Adelaide with a United States evangelist, Billy Adams, my husband saw a baby's club foot straighten out after prayer.

Years ago when my husband was preaching in Western Australia he had a word of knowledge that there were two women in the congregation who wanted children but could not have them. Two came forward and he prayed for them. We received a letter of thanks from their pastor, giving glory to God, as one woman had a baby girl 9 months after the prayer and the other had a baby girl 9 months and two weeks after the prayer.

My husband and I prayed for a couple whose first two children had died of muscular dystrophy. We met them when they had just received the news that their new baby had the same disease. We prayed earnestly that God would heal the baby but this was not to be, as he too eventually died. However, some years later when we met them again they told us that God had granted them two more children who were perfectly whole with no trace of the disease.

CHAPTER SEVEN

THREE KEYS TO FAITH

The following testimony has already appeared in the book *Discovery* in a slightly different format. Here I share three keys to my healing revealed to me by the Lord after we experienced our miracle, described below.[18]

The Key of a Deep Desire

Delight yourself in the Lord and he will give you the desires of your heart. (Ps 37:4)

The reason behind a deep desire has to be the background story that caused the desire in the first place. My husband and I had a deep love for children and had determined to have at least six, indeed we even talked jokingly of twelve! Our first baby was born and was fine except for the fact that he was jaundiced for a few days. The doctor did not seem concerned about this and as, after a few days, he improved we did not think any more of it.

When Dale was around two years I had a miscarriage. I was told to try again, and had another! Our doctor advised us to wait a while and try again later, which we did.

Our second child, Gavin, was born prematurely because of placentia praevia and died on the second day.

---

[18] Ken & Alison Chant, <u>Discovery</u>, Vision Publishing, Ramona, CA. USA. 1990 pg. 72-79.

This was a great blow to us. We could not understand why God allowed it. We grieved deeply, though Jesus became very real to us at this time and comforted us. Compassion was increased in us and after this event we were asked to pray for other grieving couples who had lost children in some way. We realised over time also that God develops spiritual power in our lives by the shaping pressures of difficult times.

We were comforted by the scripture in 2nd Corinthians 1:3-5. A wonderful scripture for anyone suffering sorrow of any kind.

Praise be to the God and Father of our Lord Jesus Christ, the Father of compassion and the God of all comfort, who comforts us in all our troubles, so that we can comfort those in any trouble with the comfort we ourselves have received from God. For just as the sufferings of Christ flow over into our lives, so also through Christ our comfort overflows.

Our desire for more children had not diminished!

Our doctor built me up physically and in time I was able to have our third child, Sharon, but I had to stay in bed throughout the pregnancy as the threat of losing her was constant. In the seventh month of my pregancy the doctor discovered I had RH negative anti-bodies, and so some of my former troubles were now exposed. Therefore when Sharon was born she was given a transfusion when only two days old.

Now I know this is no longer a problem for mothers as, with a simple injection, the antibodies that have built up in her body can be dealt with. However it is fifty years since I had my first baby and these things were not known to us then! It wasn't until my last baby was born that I was given the gamma globulin injection. What a lot of sorrow we would have been saved, but how many faith lessons Ken and I would have missed!

During my pregnancy with Sharon we were upheld by the congregation of Pastor Leo Harris. Leo was in the USA with his wife Belle and daughter Cherith, and Ken was temporarily taking care of the church in Sturt Street, Adelaide. During this time we saw many remarkable answers to prayer. The faith of that congregation was high and, Sunday after Sunday they were expecting constant miracles. I'm sure the prayers of those saints upheld us as a family at that time.

When Dale was seven and Sharon two years of age we moved to Tasmania.

Two and a half years later I had another miscarriage. This time the doctor warned that if I became pregnant again I could lose my life.

What were we to do? We were committed to the healing message and we had seen many miracles in answer to prayer. We felt we could not continue preaching the healing message while I could not have the children I so deeply desired.

I reasoned that the God who had given the desire and who had allowed me to get pregnant would surely fulfil his promises and give me more children.

So there is the background to my deep desire. The courage I needed to go on with another pregnancy was to come to me with a "rhema" word from the Lord! I made the statement to Ken that if there was someone else in the world who had RH negative blood, and I could hear their story of a miracle baby, born without difficulty, then I would feel confident that I could go ahead.

The Lord made that testimony available to me through a magazine we received in the mail. A magazine we had not sent for! The testimony I needed was there, and it was from a medical doctor, Dr William Standish Reed, which gave it great credibility.

Here is the question and answer testimony:

Question: "My wife and I have an RH incompatibility. As a result my wife has lost her last two children by miscarriages. Do you believe that we can hope to have children? Or should my wife or I have an operation to prevent any further conception?"

Answer from Dr. Reed: "A very dear friend of mine, a minister, at one time had this same problem. When his wife again conceived they faced long months of anxiety, wondering whether they would have a normal child, or even if she would be able to carry the pregnancy through to its entirety. At that time I had been studying the church's ministry of healing. I advised the minister to lay hands on his wife daily and pray in the name of Jesus of Nazareth, asking God to allow her to have a normal pregnancy and a normal child. Of course those who work out these things genetically can describe how genetic ratios can work out so that a normal child could be born but it is God who works out all these matters. Certainly man has not figured out how to juggle genes. It is my feeling that a pregnancy carried through with husband and wife praying together would produce wonderful results. The minister's wife had a normal child."

We caught hold of this wonderful testimony, it was just what we needed to give us courage to proceed with another pregnancy. Ken began to pray for me and we prayed together. It has been said there are three answers to prayer, "Yes", "No", and "Wait a while".

If God honoured our faith I knew it would truly be a miracle. According to my doctor it couldn't be done, but God did do it! This brings us to the second key:

The Key of a Steady Determination

Therefore I tell you, whatever you ask for in prayer, believe that you have received it, and it will be yours.(Mark 11:24)

So do not throw away your confidence; it will be richly rewarded. You need to persevere so that when you have done the will of God, you will receive what he has promised. (He 10:35-36)

... God who gives life to the dead and calls things that are not as though they were.(Romans 4:17)

These three verses I clung to steadily. I was determined to believe God. Grace and courage are given when they are needed, and we were given that mercy. Having a baby takes nine months and during that long time we had to keep a steady and unwavering faith.

When, at three months, I revealed my long awaited pregnancy to my doctor she was amazed! The pathologist was puzzled and tested my blood and Ken's several times, insisting it was impossible that I could be carrying an RH negative baby, (even though my husband's brother and sister were both RH negative). My bearing an RH negative baby would be the explanation of my perfect health. This would mean the baby's blood, being similar to mine, would not develop anti-bodies in my blood stream.

We walked softly before the Lord, reading the Word constantly, and encouraging each other's faith until the great day came when Eric, our fourth child, was born. Sure enough God had arranged genetically that he was RH negative like myself. He had *juggled the genes!*

The Key of Joyful Anticipation

And what is faith? Faith gives substance to our hopes, and makes us certain of realities we do not see (He 11:1, NEB).

> Faith sees the invisible, believes the incredible and receives the impossible. (Author unknown)

Our pediatrician came into the hospital to check Eric and I asked him, *"How do you account for this baby?"*. He answered me, *"We don't know, it was one in a million chance. Don't try to do it again."*

Four and a half years later God did it again and our fifth child, Baden, was born, once again RH negative.

The definition of joy, according to Webster's Dictionary, is an emotion excited by the expectation or acquisition of good. It may be experienced, even in affliction. Happiness, in contrast, rests on circumstances.

Yes, we kept an attitude of joyful anticipation, and God heard our prayers. He *"juggled the genes"* making it possible for us to have the two babies who now of course have children of their own!

<u>There was one caution to our faith</u>: We were continually seeking God and his glory, not just healing for ourselves. If we had not received our "rhema" word in the testimony from Dr Reed, and had we not also both "received" Romans 4:17, which in particular spoke to Ken more than Dr. Reed's article, we would not have gone ahead with a pregnancy as that would have been testing the Lord which we are forbidden to do. Our hope always is in the Lord and in him alone. We are his servants and he can do with us as seems good in his sight.

Since these events, and the lessons of faith we were taught through them, I have met many other women of faith who prayed similar prayers and were also granted children because of the Lord's great mercy and goodness.

If we delight ourselves in the Lord and show a steady determination to do his will and believe him for healing, then we will be filled with joy as we wait for him to move in our lives.

But may all who seek you rejoice and be glad in you; may those who love your salvation always say,'The Lord be exalted.' (Ps 40:16)

Surgery of the Soul

Three years after Eric's birth Dr Reed published a book on healing – *Surgery of the Soul* – which we found very helpful in our ministry to the sick. His book came out of twenty - three years of study on the matter of healing and how it relates to the whole man. He has some very interesting things to say about healing: [19]

> It is my position at this point to state that our patients cannot become whole without Jesus Christ. There is no other philosophical system or religion which gives honour to the eternal spirit of man or which shows him the means of personal salvation and the way to wholeness and to life eternal which compares in any way to Christianity. We who read scientific literature to such a demanding degree should realise that great insight into the persons of our patients and ourselves can be derived through the reading and study of the Holy Bible. Jesus Christ has much to say to us, the physicians of today.
>
> The gospel truth needs to be taken from the churches and from the pages of the NT and lived out in the lives of believers, particularly those who profess and call themselves Christians. **Were those who profess Christianity to begin to believe it, and to live it, certainly the world would know it within twenty four hours.**

"Jesus said unto her, I am the resurrection and the life; he that believeth in me, though he were dead, yet shall he live." (Jn 11:25)

---

[19] Dr. William Standish Reed, Surgery of the Soul, Fleming H. Revell Co. 1969. pg. 29-30 & 79-80.

If the power of Jesus' resurrection is such, believers today should know what this power is. It should not be allowed to lie fallow in the institutional Church; it should be applied in the lives of those who are Christians. This is particualrly true for those who are in the practice of medicine or nursing or surrounded with difficult and ofttimes impossible situations which in human terms are incurable or unimprovable. If Jesus Christ is God, and if his power is undiminished today, he who said that he would never leave us or forsake us, will be the factor in transforming the hopeless times of life into his Divine and glorious hope.

The Wonder and the Mystery of Divine Healing
Alison Chant

CHAPTER EIGHT

THE HEALING COVENANT

The mystery of why some are healed and some are not could lie in part in the Old Testament covenant of healing that God made with ancient Israel.

Can we expect God to heal if we take no notice of his advice?

While we know, as born again Christians, we are not under law but under grace, there are sensible suggestions in Leviticus chapter eleven that we would do well to heed. Such as not eating any scavenger. God in his wisdom considers those animals who are scavengers unclean and not fit to eat.

Apart from this consideration there are many reasons for sickness in our present world even for those of us who are believers and have faith in God's healing power.

Our way of life has diverged far from the rural lifestyle enjoyed by our forebears. Wrong living has been foisted on us by our industrial society, and the long distances between work and home and the faster pace of modern living add to the stress of modern life.

Our soil and water are polluted, modern farming methods have added to the poisonous blend and there is no longer the same goodness in the soil to be absorbed by the plants we eat.

Added to this is the tendency to deliberately destroy our health with fast food, carbonated drinks, smoking, alcohol and other deadly substances.

Even if we turn aside from these temptations our bodies must still contend with fruit and vegetables picked green for marketing purposes so that they lack the nutrients God intended.

Dr Don Colbert writes in his book *Toxic Relief*:[20]

> We live in a toxic world – a toxic planet that is taking its toll on our bodies every day, whether we know it or not. Due to our technological advances since the Industrial Revolution, we have continued to pour dangerous chemicals and pollutants into our streams, soil and air. At this moment, you probably have some amount of lead in your body, usually stored in your bones – all of us do. Most of us have small amounts of DDT (or its metabolite DDE, which is what it changes into during metabolism) in our fatty tissues.

Then, on top of all this, there is more stress on our bodies caused by the breakdown of the family unit, and the high incidence of divorce. This brings a subsequent strain on the nuclear family, which is added to by the knowledge we gain through television of the state of our world, with its wars and famines. Recently the murderous threat of terrorism, now a spectre facing us all, has added more stress to modern living.

---

20 Dr. Don Colbert, Toxic Relief, Publisher, Siloam A. Strang Co. 2001. pg. 6.

Toward Health and Happiness

Considering all the things that can cause modern sicknesses there is a lot we can do for ourselves before asking God to heal us!

We can be careful not to neglect rest and recreation. We can eat intelligently, trying to stay within the foods available in our area according to the season. We can eat and drink as close to natural products as possible, avoiding those things that are adulterated in any way.

This year, at the Sydney Gardening Show, Peter Cundell, star of the television programme – *Gardening Australia* – was heard to boast that he had reached the age of seventy eight without any arthritis, high blood pressure, heart disease or any other disease because he eats fresh garden produce that he grows himself without using any poisonous substances.

Growing them gives him the exercise he needs and picking them straight from his own garden guarantees their freshness.

If we continue to poison ourselves by wrong eating and wrong living then can we expect God to heal us?

If we know the truth but don't take heed to change our lifestyle then we are guilty. It seems to me that God is not lavish with his miracles but sparing of them in our land. This may be because of our lack of faith, or perhaps God sees more need among the poor and destitute of this world than he does in we who belong to today's comparitively rich western society. We do after all have pain medication drugs for physical troubles, and innoculations for our children easily available to us.

With these things in mind if we need healing then the first thing we need to do is repent of our wrong attitudes and life-style and make a firm decision to change our ways before we can believe God to bring healing miracles into our life. This is common sense as, even if in his mercy God should heal us, our continuing to live wrongly will cause the sickness to return again.

In *Toxic Relief* Dr. Colbert also advocates fasting as a natural principle of healing: [21]

> Think about it: When an animal is injured or sick, what does it do? It finds a resting place where it can lap up water, and it quits eating while it heals. This is natural, instinctual wisdom that God placed within the animal kingdom.
>
> But when we get sick, what do we do?
>
> When we get sick with an injury or illness, such as pneumonia, a sinus infection or strep throat, instead of resting and fasting and drinking water or juices only, we eat ice-cream, puddings, creamy soups and other rich, high-caloric foods that do nothing to cleanse and detoxify the body.

Dealing with pressures of modern living is a somewhat harder battle but there are many self help books dealing with stress and how to overcome the rush and hurry of

---

[21] Ibid. pg. 46-47

our world. Below are a few from my own shelves. [22]

My eldest brother, James McIntyre, who is now seventy nine years of age and a retired pastor, has learned how to discipline his body. In a recent letter he told me, *"If I hadn't been called to Christian ministry I would have been very happy to be a naturopath!"* Here are some extracts from his letter written on 14th October 2005.

Extracts From James' Letter

My first wake up call was when a pastor during the 80's I found myself getting puffed out while preaching. I realised I was sitting down studying, sitting down counselling, and sitting down talking on the phone. So I started walking...

About this time I had an experience along the lines that God wanted me to have a strong body so he could use me in the years to come. I began regular fasting and longer walks...

Then in 1991 I found I couldn't read. All I could see on the page was a brown fog! I couldn't get up for several days as I felt extremely dizzy. I received a fright and joined a gymnasium and began training, lifting weights. My eyesight recovered after a week

---

[22] Charles L. Allen, God's Psychiatry, Fleming H. Revell, Grand Rapids. MI. USA. 1953. Don Hawkins Th.M., Frank Mirnirth M.D., Paul Meier M.D. & Chris Thurman, Ph.D. Before Burnout, The Moody Bible Institute, Chicago. Ill. USA. 1990. Dr. Henry Cloud & Dr. John Townsend, Boundaries at Home, Strand Publishing, Sydney Australia. 2002. Dr. Janet Hall, Fight Free Families, A Lothian Book. Port Melbourne. Victoria. 1994. Robert M. Hicks, The Christian Family in Changing Times, Baker Books. Grand Rapids. MI. USA. 2002.

of the gymnasium training! I have belonged to a gymnasium ever since.

God can give us health supernaturally and he can also give us the power to keep our bodies disciplined.

Initially I had hoped that there was a supernatural free gift of health, like salvation and sanctification. The Holy Spirit gives me the answer to indwelling sin in Romans chapter eight so why not a scripture for continuous health? First Corinthians 9:27 showed me that I have to exercise and take care of my body and it's all about self denial.

No, I beat my body and make it my slave so that after I have preached to others, I myself will not be disqualified for the prize.

The bottom line for me is if I can't think I can't pray, so I try to live in such a way that my brain gets oxygen and an unpolluted blood supply. I've amassed one hundred and sixty books on health Some of the best are about the nature cure movement, started by Christian doctors and usually called the *Natural Hygiene Movement*. Paul Bragg and Professor Ehret were great advocates.

Lee Bueno, who wrote *Fast Your Way to Health*, is one of the leaders in the Christian nature cure movement. She and her husband are Pentecostal evangelists.[23]

There are ten thousand of these people around the world who demonstrate perfect health, even into old age, and I read their books and get encouraged to remain alive and well.

Sick people are the result of the modern machine age. One hundred years ago our body and our horse did all the work. Now we can live without any exercise. We can even go shopping in a little motorised go-cart, but we were built for motion.

I know a Spirit filled naturopath in Queensland who used to minister to the sick and deliver people from Satanic bondage. But, the sick, after being healed, kept getting sick again. So now he teaches Christians how to live a healthy life style. This is the world we live in!

But the remarkable thing is how well we are! We are hard to kill. On the whole we live a good life. I have never had a serious illness apart from the 'flu, I don't even get headaches as I have fasted many times throughout my life. God is good. (*James McIntyre*)

Will God heal mental illness?

There is a great proliferation of mental ill health in our day. I believe one of the reasons is an abandonment of the

---

[23] Lee Bueno, <u>Fast Your Way to Health</u>, Whitaker House; 1991 (Contact: Born Again Body Inc. P.O. Box 969, Calistoga, CA. 94515 USA.)

Judeo/Christian ethic that was taught automatically to children in the past. Humanism, strange new beliefs, and experimentation in recreational drugs by so many young people have led to an explosion of mental illness.

Added to this is the fact of the breakdown of family life so that many have no role models to teach them how to live, make decisions, or look ahead to the results that will accrue from the way they are living in the present.

Unregenerate man thinks mainly of self, and up to sixty-seventy five percent of those who are emotionally sick are seeking release from bondages of fear, anxiety and worry. Through a lifetime of negative thinking and habit patterns they are slowly but surely brought into these crippling bondages.

Many with mild to severe mental health problems can be helped far more readily by accepting Christ as Saviour, confessing their sins to God and making things right with their neighbour than they can from many prolonged sessions with a psychiatrist. If we would follow the commandment of Jesus we would lay the groundwork for complete mental health.

Love the Lord your God with all your heart and all your soul and with all your mind. This is the first and greatest command-ment. And the second is like it. Love your neighbour as yourself. All the law and the prophets hang on these two command-ments. (Mt 22:37-40)

The psychiatrist Dr. Carl Jung advocated primary knowledge of God. Shortly before he died he was asked directly whether he believed there is a God and he said, "No, I do not believe, I know." Jung's father and eight uncles were ministers of the gospel and he believed people could be helped by finding a religious outlook on life, but he decried the fact that so many clergymen had nothing but empty words to give to those who were suffering from a twisted view of life. This, he felt, was because they were too taken up with doctrine at the expense of a close relationship with God himself. Today, thankfully there are many Christian pastors who have been trained, not only in the Word of God, but in counselling so that they are well able to help people in trouble.

> Jung had a deep and abiding respect for the Bible and saw it as a book that speaks of the meaning of life, the meaning of death and of the mysteries of evil and suffering as well as the mysteries of love and healing. It deals with the psychic fact of sin and guilt and the liberation that comes with forgiveness. Above all it deals with the holy, with the realities that are beyond words and simple formulations...for Jung the psyche/soul is the place where the divine and human intersect. He understood that Christ was the divine model of that intersection. He also affirmed that the cross is the most appropriate symbol of that intersection between the vertical and the horizontal and that it represents the need for the ego to die so the soul could come to life. [24]

Can Christians suffer emotional problems?

Christians can suffer emotional problems and these

---

[24] David G. Benner (Ed.), Baker's Encyclopedia of Psychology, Baker Book House, Grand Rapids, MI. USA. 1985. pg. 165

people must be taught to set their minds on the things of God as Jesus is the remedy for all soul problems.

It is the curse of our modern age with its frenetic activity that we so seldom take time to think long eternal thoughts about God, eternity, our personal goals, and the direction we want our life to take.

Since you have been raised with Christ, set your hearts on things above, where Christ is seated at the right hand of God. Set your mind on things above, not on earthly things, for you died, and your life is now hidden with Christ in God. (Cl 3:1-3)

Learning about Jesus our Saviour through his Word, and believing we are safely hidden with him in God will protect us from anxious fears.

Christians who have accepted Christ as Saviour have the Holy Spirit indwelling them and they must learn to trust God, to meditate in his Word, and to walk each day in the strength of the Holy Spirit.

When doubts intrude they must be taught to set them aside by looking to Jesus the author and finisher of their faith (He 12:2), and to the cross where he overcame Satan (Re 1:17-18), and all his evil hosts who go about seeking to oppress and torment Christians. The Apostle Peter warns us:

Be self-controlled and alert. Your enemy the devil prowls around like a roaring lion looking for someone to devour. Resist him, standing firm in the faith. (1 Pe 5:8-9a)

It is only as we stand firm in our faith, resisting the devil, believing that God is in control and that we can safely trust in his saving power that we can gain the victory we need.

What are some of the symptoms of emotional problems that can attack Christians and what is the remedy?

The symptoms are uncontrolled thoughts, lack of concentration when reading the Word of God, unanswered prayer, and doubts about salvation. Sufferers may have a

tension band around their head, a fear of losing control, thoughts of suicide, fear of being alone, fear of losing their mind, and the like.

Jesus said, *"Let not your heart be troubled, neither let it be afraid,"* (Jn 14:27) Christians who are fearful must learn to trust God and not allow cares, anxieties and troubled thoughts to become dominant in their life.

Does it do any good to pray for these people or is it more productive to teach them where they are going wrong in their understanding of the Christian life?

We should certainly pray for them but also teach them that if they labour for God in their own strength, for self gratification, and not for the glory of God, and in the strength of the Holy Spirit, then they will become emotionally exhausted and be open to nervous troubles.

If they have stopped reading the Word of God, and they no longer pray, then they will eventually weaken their trust in God, in the atonement, and in all that Jesus won for them on the cross.

The result is spiritual malnutrition which means their resistance is lowered and the devil finds them an easy mark.

The way to healing for these troubles is for the person to repent, turn around, and seek the Lord earnestly. They must re-establish their relationship with God by returning to meditation in the Word of God, coupled with prayer. The Lord delights to give revelation knowledge to those who diligently study his Word and pray for enlightenment. (Ep 1:15-23)

The writer to the Hebrews warns about falling away from the faith:

We have much to say about this but it is hard to explain because you are slow to learn. In fact, though by this time you ought to be teachers, you need someone to teach you the elementary truths of God's word all over again. You need milk, not solid food! Anyone who lives on milk, being still an infant, is not acquainted with the teaching about right-eousness. But solid food is for the mature, who by constant use have trained themselves to distinguish good from evil. (He 5:11-14)

So as well as prayer these people need teaching. If the Christian has had emotional troubles for many years then his/her whole thinking pattern will have to change, I John 1:8-9 and Romans 12:1-2 should be studied carefully.

CHAPTER NINE

MORE WONDERFUL HEALINGS

While we were living in the USA, Pastor Joe Higgins, of San Diego, California told us of his youth growing up in the city of Zion, established by the healing evangelist Alexander Dowie in 1899. There were no theatres or hotels in the city and no one worked on Sundays. This has changed today as Zion is now just the same as any ordinary American city. Joe remembers Zion Temple with rows and rows of wheel chairs, crutches, sticks, and other aids lining the walls, left by grateful people who were healed under Dowie's ministry. As far as he can recall everyone he saw Dowie pray for was healed. Those who were not healed immediately Dowie would take aside to repent of some sin in their life. Then, when he prayed for them again, they too would be healed. Altogether many thousands of people claimed to be healed under Dowie's ministry.

It seems from Dowie on there was an increasing interest in the healing power of God. At this time also the Holy Spirit began to be poured out both in Kansas, under Charles Parham and then later in Azusa St, Los Angeles, under William J. Seymour. With the outpouring of the Holy Spirit came a further interest in the power of God to heal the sick, and many great ministries sprang up to preach the healing gospel and pray for the sick in the name of Jesus the Great Physician. From then until now many thousands of great miracles of healing have occurred.

When I first thought of writing down my thoughts on the mystery that seems to surround God's healing message I began collecting testimonies from different people to add to this book.

Here is a remarkable testimony from the year 1936. Pastor Stephen Dowling of the Assembly of God has given me permission to share his story which I will give in full as written by himself.

This Sickness is Not Unto Death

Is the Day of Miracles Past? (This) was the title of a 1936 tract written by my mother as a testimony to my experience of God's incredible healing power and marvellous grace. I, for one, can personally affirm that the day of miracles has not passed and that God's word is true...Jesus Christ is the same, yesterday, today and forever (He 13:8).

So, for the glory of God, and his glory alone, I share my testimony of God's mighty healing power in my life.

A Mother's Faith

First, I would like to praise God for a godly mother – Melva Dowling – now deceased and in the presence of her Lord. Her salvation was the result of the ministry of Pastor Phillip Duncan, who wonderfully ministered to her in the midst of a marriage breakdown back in the early thirties.

My mother's faith in Christ never wavered although her faith cost her separation, despair, and much suffering. She was a source of much inspiration to many people over the years, especially to me. Because of her life I am in the ministry today.

After the marriage break-up my mother left Sydney where I was born, and we went to live with my grandmother in Melbourne. They attended Richmond Temple, now Richmond Assembly of God.

Paralysed, Blind and Dumb

On August 4, 1934, at six years of age I was suddenly struck down with encephalitis lethargica, a deadly germ that affects the spinal cord and eventually destroys the cells of the brain. This disease left me completely paralysed, blind, dumb, unable to eat, the cells of the brain destroyed, and in a coma for over 12 months in the Children's Hospital, Melbourne.

When I took seriously ill the late Pastor C. L. Greenwood called the church to fasting and prayer for my healing. By this time my whole body was wasted away almost to nothing with the bones clearly seen through the flesh. The hospital specialists told my mother that if I ever came out of the coma I would be mentally retarded for the rest of my life. In fact, they registered me with the Kew Asylum, Melbourne.

Praise God this was not to be so, for as the saints began to pray, God began to work in my body. I slowly came out of the coma, although the doctors still affirmed that I had but a little time to live.

A Sure Word From God

At this time my mother went to do domestic work for a Church of England minister by the name of Rev. Kent, with whom my mother shared on the blessedness of the Baptism of the Holy Spirit.

One morning in 1936 the phone rang at the manse and my mother answered. It was the hospital to say that there was no hope of recovery and, if mother wished, she could take me home to die. Suddenly the Lord spoke to my mother these words: *'This sickness is not unto death, but for the glory of God'*.

At that instant Rev. Kent came out of his study and asked, *'Was that the Children's Hospital?'* My mother replied, yes, and Rev. Kent said, *'I have had a strange experience, as if God is saying to me this sickness is not unto death, but for the glory of God'*. God had confirmed to both of them that He was about to perform a healing in my body!

God Performs the Miracle

Promptly they phoned Pastor Greenwood and together they collected me from the hospital and took me to my grandparent's home in Caulfield, not to die, but to be raised up in perfect health.

Both Pastor Greenwood and Rev. Kent prayed for me before they left and mother, believing for full recovery, immediately put her faith into operation and began to force feed milk to me, a teaspoon at a time, in the mighty name of Jesus. Praise God, he gradually began to loosen up my paralysed limbs, gave sight to my eyes and speech to my tongue. God performed a miracle and I was able to return to school.

As my mother wrote in a testimony tract in April, 1936: *'God, in answer to prayer raised the child up, put flesh on his bones, gave sight to his blind eyes, speech to his tongue, power to walk and run in his paralysed limbs, and removed the destroyed cells in his brain...this healing is not a process of nature; it is a work of God...'*

Doctors Amazed

From the age of eleven until I was thirteen, I was often called into the Children's Hospital to be examined by overseas doctors who read the history of my illness and were amazed at the remarkable recovery but would never acknowledge that it was the work of God.

I will ever be grateful to God for his mercy and goodness to me. God has blessed me with a lovely wife and a family of three married daughters who worship at Northside Christian Centre, Bundoora, and a son who worships at Richmond AOG. My wife and I are presently pioneering a work in Sunbury, Victoria.

May this testimony be a source of encouragement to believe God for great things in your life. (*Stephen Dowling*)

What an amazing testimony this is from Pastor Dowling and how gracious is our God. This was a definite miracle of God's divine intervention, honouring the faith of a woman of God, the pastors concerned, and also the church people who prayed and fasted for this young boy who was to prove a true man of God. Faith was there, the people involved agreed together for his healing and Stephen's mother acted out her faith by feeding him small amounts of milk until he was able to eat solid food.

Coming forward forty years to 1977, here is another testimony told to me by Frank Holland, who attends our home church, New Horizons Community Church, St. Mary's, Sydney, under Pastor Grant Redman.

Frank Holland's Testimony

In 1977 while working for Crane, Australia, I was given the task of painting valves using special paint thinner for painting off-shore rigging. This special thinner was to keep the valves dry and stop corrosion from the salty sea air.

While mixing the paint with the thinner some splashed on my arms. I knew the thinner had to be washed off with soap and water within one minute and I did wash with water. However there was no soap available and as there were only a few minutes to go before I knocked off I finished what I was doing before getting to the soap. By then it was too late and by the next morning I had developed contact dermatitis on my arms and hands and my feet also swelled up to two sizes larger and stayed that way for the next two years.

Over those two years the affected areas continually broke out in blisters and weeping dermatitis. I could not close my fists and this made driving difficult and dangerous.

I was taken off the painting work and given a job in stores which involved using a forklift, also very dangerous because of my lack of a firm grip.

I was not a Christian at this time but a Christian fellow worker, Bill Oldroyd, began telling me that God loved me and cared about me.

On September 1st I was invited to a prayer meeting where Pastor Ken Tydeman offered to pray for my dermatitis and after the prayer Ken invited me to give my heart to the Lord.

His exact words to me were, *'Now you have been healed would you like to give your heart to the Lord?'*

I looked at my arms and said, *'I'm not healed yet, there is no sign of healing, but OK, I will give my heart to the Lord.'*

During the night, at around 2.00 a.m., I woke with a burning sensation in my arms. I ran my hands under the cold tap, rewrapped them in fresh bandages and went back to bed. An hour later I felt the burning again but decided to do no more until morning. I slept again and in the morning, some nine hours from the time of the prayer the night before, woke to find my arms with perfectly normal skin. My feet also suddenly reduced to their normal size so that I had to buy new shoes.

> Since then I have trusted the Lord for healing many times but none has been so spectacular as my healing from the devastation made by the paint thinner! *(Frank Holland)*

This remarkable testimony shows the prayer of faith being offered for an unbeliever; the point of contact was made and Frank's faith was challenged. He acted out his faith by agreeing to accept the Lord as his Saviour even though he could not yet see any improvement. God honoured the faith of the people praying together, Ken Tydeman's faith, Frank's faith, and the faith of the others at the meeting. Together they reached out for the healing power of God who graciously completed Frank's healing during the night.

This next testimony comes from another member of the same church. I see her on a regular basis and can attest to the truth of her testimony.

Helen Leek's Testimony

> At twenty three years of age I had been a Christian for five years. Brought up in the Methodist Church in Forbes, I attended the Presbyterian Church in Wagga during my college years. The 60's and 70's were a time of charismatic renewal in the mainline churches of Australia and the minister of the Forbes Methodist church was filled with the Holy Spirit. During my holidays in 1974 he invited a team from YWAM to come to Forbes to hold coffee shops to attract young people in to discuss the gospel. It was at this time that I received the Holy Spirit. I did not have the witness of speaking in tongues at that time but felt a definite anointing.

One year later I did receive the gift of tongues and have been rejoicing in that experience ever since.

In 1977 I had a smallpox vaccination which caused encephalitis from which epilepsy resulted. I had had a petit mal seizure before this vaccination but the encephalitis greatly exacerbated the problem and caused not only petit mal, but grand mal seizures.

Because of the encephalitis I was in and out of hospital for one year and was finally put on medication for the grand mal seizures. Unfortunately the medication did not stabilize my condition, nor was the level of the medication in my blood stable. I had a very short attention span, unable to remember more than two lines of news print at a time.

I met Warren, my husband, at the Anglican Church in Canterbury and we married in 1981. To our sorrow we were advised not to try to have any children because of my epilepsy and the medication I had to take. This was a time of great trouble for us, sometimes I would go out shopping or visiting, collapse, and finish the day in hospital on medication to try to bring the epilepsy under control.

In 1982 desperate because of the insecurity of my life, not knowing from day to day whether I would have a seizure or not, and then having to put up with the aftermath of the seizure, which was equally horrible, I cried out to God in prayer.

Lying in bed one night, praying earnestly, I received a word from God. His words were not audible to my ears but nevertheless they were very real to me. So much so that I had no hesitation in obeying the words that came into my mind and heart. The word God spoke to me was that I was healed, and I was to throw away my medication, which I did! I slept really well that night because my heart was full of faith. My poor husband slept very poorly though, as he was full of concern for me.

Twenty five years have passed since that night and I have had no more fits. I was able to go on then to the next step of faith and to discontinue my contraceptive pill. I became pregnant and then went to my doctor to tell him of my healing and also that I was pregnant.

Doctor Gabrael was sympathetic and had no trouble believing that something wonderful had indeed happened to me. Over the years since then God has blessed us with two daughters and a son. Our son is currently a swimming champion and recently won six gold medals in Germany.

Since my healing my memory has vastly improved, I have successfully sat exams to become a Technical Official for swimming races; came second in the examination for National Training for Royal Rangers, and am currently attending a Bible College and running a Bible study for my church. (*Helen Leek*)

This testimony of healing is very different to Frank's. Helen, because she was already a Christian, received a 'rhema' word from the Lord which she bravely put into practice. This is one of those times when God moves sovereignly for one of his children. The timing of this miracle is significant. It occurred during the charismatic renewal when God was moving in healing to a remarkable degree. Faith was high and many people were experiencing the healing power of God for the first time.

However I would not personally advocate anyone throwing away their medication. There have been cases of people who have misguidedly stopped taking the medication recommended by a physician with tragic results. It is far better to let your doctor tell you that you are healed and no longer need the medication he formerly recommended.

The Wonder and the Mystery of Divine Healing
Alison Chant

CHAPTER TEN

A JOURNEY TO WHOLENESS

The following testimony was written by a unique individual named Tex who never attended school and did not learn to read and write properly until he became a Christian. He grew up in the Australian 'outback' and, after his parents died, he managed to escape going to school and worked as a 'jackaroo' from the age of ten years. When he finally became a Christian his friends discovered that, because he had lived in the remote outback all his life, he was not registered as a citizen of Australia. However with help he was able to remedy this problem. After a tremendous born again experience he conceived a desire to learn about his Saviour and began with God's help to learn to read and write more accurately.

When Tex first applied to Vision Bible College he had been rejected by some other Bible Colleges in Australia because of his lack of education. We felt led to give him the opportunity he so much desired, to learn all he could about the Christian life, and about the Lord he had learned to love. He did well, and within four years he had gained his Diploma in Theology. One of the essays he wrote for us embodies his full testimony and all the wonderful things God did for him, He has a unique style and some colourful language and we were so impressed with his story that I promised to add it to this book. Perhaps as you read Tex's unusual testimony you will agree that God delights on picking up the downtrodden and setting them on their feet to glorify his name. He stands behind his word to perform it!

Some of his outback phraseology will sound strange to you so I will add a glossary of terms at the end of this chapter.

A Wonderful Healing

When the daily train from the 'big smoke', arrived at 'Elbow on the River' at midday, amid the cold chilly winds and rains of the winter of 1982, amongst the many passengers to disembark was myself, Tex Quicksilver. I was noticed, not because of my importance, but because Murray River towns of South Australia, such as this one, had not since the late 1800's seen a stranger clad as I was.

For, although my walk was of a man in deep pain, attention could not help being drawn to me also because of my outfit. I was wearing my usual clothing for the winter, a black oilskin, a Stetson hat, elastic sided boots, with a 'swag' wrapped in a 'bluey' slung across my back. From my left shoulder to my right hip, I carried a stirrup leather, while in my right hand was a walking cane. A stock whip coiled over my right shoulder while my left supported a worn saddle showing years of hard use. Walking at my left side was a dog, showing in its bearing no tolerance of strangers.

I had come down from the north, near the Barcoo River, country of black soil plains and 'brigalow' scrub. According to my doctor I had only six months to live.

The Wonder and the Mystery of Divine Healing
Alison Chant

Hiding my pain I slowly made my way to the local police station, where I accepted a ride to my place of destination. I had come here to die, to spend my last months with my faithful 'track mate'. But life doesn't always go the way we would like it. The office was closed! I waited impatiently, some twenty minutes passed and still no one came to open the office. Then through the rain and wind a rider on a horse approached and reined in close to me

The rider was a young girl, only fourteen years of age, yet she sat her pony, despite the storm around her, as a veteran of much older years. She explained to me that the office would not open that day as the owner had gone to a football match! Would I like a hot drink and a meal at her parents unit? Still wary, I accepted her offer. Imagine my shock when she told me she was a Christian and that she hoped I was O.K.

There were two peoples I had no time for. The first was fancy folk, with their fancy talk, and their soft hands; and second was 'Bible thumpers' and 'sky pilots'. Fancy folk, because they always speak as if they are smarter than anyone else, 'Bible thumpers' and 'sky pilots', because, I thought, they were always trying to get me to give up wild women, drinking, smoking, and gambling, these being the only real pleasures I had in life!

But little was I to know that God moves in many different ways, and so it was for me, for as one journey ends another begins! **I had come to**

'Elbow on the River' to die, but God had seen I was directed here to live!

By a Fire of Gidgee Coals

That night, I was in a caravan where I had shut and locked the door against the winter wind and rain. My whiskey was all gone and there was only some coffee and tobacco for myself and a few dry stale biscuits for my 'track mate'. None of the stores would be open until Monday, I said to my dog *"It could be worse, at least we're both dry, old mate."*

Then, placing my smashed up right side in a comfortable position I mused in reflection about how it only seemed like yesterday when a great horse had rolled on me. I remembered how the doctors said by all accounts I should have been dead. I remembered also how I had bragged to those doctors and nurses that no horse or bullock had yet been bred that was tougher than me! I was told at the time I would never walk again, but defied the odds and did! *"Yep old mate", I said to the dog, "it could have been worse, but we made it, hey."*

So I mused and reflected on the trips down the long paddocks. I had travelled from Curry to the Towers; from the Towers to Alexandria Downs in the Territory; from the Fink River to the Lake Everglades; from the Gulf to the Georgia Plains.

I thought of the mates I had made along the way and of quart pots and fires of 'gidgee' coals. Of the nights the mobs would break and rush, of the headlong dash in the night, sometimes bright with moonlight, other nights black as a sinner's heart.

This was the way life was meant to be; sure legs got broken, and bodies got gored occasionally by a 'brigelow scrubber'. Arms were broken and cracked, and broken ribs and feet were suffered, but this was all part and parcel of life as a 'Jackaroo'.

God's Timing is Perfect

At that point in time I knew nothing of God or his humour and sense of timing! However hearing a knock I opened the door, and what did I see but a 'Bible thumper' who asked me if I would like to go to church.

"No way", I replied. Then he told me there was supper after the service. I was hungry and I knew that when a man's belly was screaming louder than a mad cut snake he had to swallow his pride, so with bile churning, I reluctantly entered the car. On the way the driver asked me if I had ever been to church or if I was a Christian! *"No way,"* I replied.

Little did I know there was someone sitting by my side having a big chuckle, because before that night was done he was going to become a very special 'mate' to me. His name was Jesus and he was sitting in the back seat of the car as it headed for Victor Harbour.

This was the beginning of my journey to wholeness through Jesus Christ.

The Wonder and the Mystery of Divine Healing
Alison Chant

Only as I stepped into the Gospel Centre's lights was it seen that here was a dead man walking. I was gaunt and wasted and barely able to move. I stepped outside into the shadows and rolled myself a smoke amidst stony stares, which I totally ignored. When finished I slowly made my way to a rear pew where I could sit and nap as the show started. If only I'd known what God had in store!

When the singing stopped, I was awakened by a voice that caught my attention. I looked to the front and saw a man who stood about six feet tall, but it wasn't his height or his dress that caught my attention, but the message he was speaking. The man's name was Don Glazbrook and his message was, 'God's Amazing Grace'!

When he closed his message he asked if anyone present would like to come down and rededicate their life to Jesus, or if anyone sick, or lame, wanted to come down for healing. Was there anyone there who would like to receive Jesus into their life?

God Gets My Attention

I was laughing now at the people heading to the front of the church. My attention was focussed on the food that I had seen set out in a side room! As I sat there laughing to myself and thinking what a bunch of sheep these people were, **I felt a cracking, like a bull whip, across and down my back.** It felt like a fire, a fire which I was later to know as the 'Fire of the Holy Spirit'! Before I knew what was happening, because I could only move slowly at the best of times, I found myself first in the line at the front.

As I stood waiting I saw appear before me a light, and in that light I saw a man I was soon to know as Jesus, King of Kings. Then I saw two roads, one long and narrow and the other short and broad. On the narrow road I saw many pot holes, trip wires and prickly pear. On the broad but short road, I saw only darkness. Then Jesus, the man I could see in the vision, spoke to me and said, *"The choice is yours. Walk the narrow road to my Father's Heavenly Kingdom and I will also walk with you! Or you can stay on the broad short road you are now on. What is your choice? Will you be my disciple and follow after me? Will you take up this cross daily in my name, or will you continue on the path you have walked for all these years? The choice is yours tonight!"*

For the first time in my life I felt tears welling up, not since I was ten had I felt this kind of emotion and as I went to wipe away the tears I felt a hand on my shoulder and a voice asking, *"What would you like prayer for?"* Without hesitation, because I was no fool, I said, *"I want to give myself to Jesus!"* Then as pastor Don Glazbrook prayed, this tough old bushman wept! My tears flowed like living waters and I felt the love of Jesus come over me, a sinner worse than most, and I felt that Jesus wept too as he smiled and took me into his arms and heart.

There was great rejoicing in the heavenlies as the angels gave thanksgiving for one more soul, for it had indeed been a hard slog to this place of victory. He who was once lost was now found, he who was once blind, now could see, he who was once bound, now was free. I had taken the second step to victory over death.

As I had never owned or read a Bible in my life, and being self taught in the reading of letters and words, I borrowed, after much asking around, a picture Bible. That night I began seeking through this picture Bible, God's truth, and the beginning of my journey to wholeness of spirit, soul, body and mind!

I asked Pastor Don could I be 'dipped and branded'. Pastor Don replied that I would first have to learn ten lessons about baptism and then answer questions about why I wanted to be a new man. This was standard procedure for everyone who wanted to be baptised so I learned the lessons and after ten days was anxious to be 'dipped and branded' as soon as possible. After all, the specialist, who had told me of my blood disease, had said I only had six months to live and I wanted to make sure that I was alright with my Maker before I went to push up prickly pear and 'spinifex'!

Finally, three weeks later, arrangements were made for me to be baptised on a Sunday evening the 17th June at 7.30 p.m. On the Wednesday before that weekend I went to see my specialist for more tests and more bad news about my blood disease.

The Wonder and the Mystery of Divine Healing
Alison Chant

Amazing Grace

But now the Sunday evening had finally arrived and folk were gathering around for the service. I was asked what hymn I would like as I entered the waters to be 'dipped and branded'. I chose 'Amazing Grace' and some amazing things were now to occur. As I entered the warm waters of the large tub I was held by Pastor Don, Bruce Walters, and Bruce Golding. I had a support on my right leg and arm and also on my back, where it had been broken in two places when I had been rolled by that horse. But now incredible events were to happen as I lay in the water, being prayed for as "Amazing Grace" was sung by the congregation.

I felt two angels come and lift me out of the water. In reality, as I looked back, I could see myself still in the water, Jesus also appeared in this vision and said, *"When you emerge from these waters you will no longer be as you are now."* Then I felt I was gently placed back into the water. At this moment of time I received the baptism of the Holy Spirit and spoke out in other tongues and I came out of the waters, removing as I did so the supports from my right leg and right arm, and my back. Amazing grace! Amazing love!

Healed of a Blood Disease

Three days after my baptism I had to return to the specialist; three times that day they removed blood from my body for testing. Three times they came back puzzled and confused because the meltdown of the blood tissues, which is life threatening, had gone and my blood was now completely normal.

Can you picture my jubilation! I arrived back at "Elbow on the River" at 7.00 p.m. and rang my newly found friends to proclaim the good news. *"I am healed, praise Jesus"!*

This message I can bear witness to today as fourteen years have passed since my journey to wholeness first began. (*John (Texas) Bryan Quicksilver*).

Glossary:

Outback – remote area of Australia

Jackaroo – outback Australian cowboy.

Elbow on the River – The aboriginal name for the town of Goolwa.

Big Smoke – the City.

Swag and bluey – a bed roll and blanket.

Brigalow scrub – acacia trees.

Brigalow scrubber – wild cattle.

Track mate – faithful dog

Bible thumpers – Christians who witness.

Sky Pilots – Pastors.

Long Paddocks – Roadways used to move stock, especially for the grass on either side.

Mate – friend.

Gidgee coals – Stumps from any of several acacia trees from the dryer parts of Australia.

Dipped and branded – Baptised in water. (analogous with the dipping and branding of sheep).

Spinifex – tough, tussocky grass.

There were two things about this testimony that touched me. One was that Jesus, realising that Tex had had no schooling was gracious to give him a vision to explain what he needed to do to be born again. And second, as a counsellor, I realised that Tex's tears were caused by the fact that his emotions had frozen when his parents died and he had bravely striven to care for himself from the age of ten years. The tears he shed were proof of the healing taking place in his emotions as the Lord made up to him for the lonely years he spent growing up in the rough, tough world of the Australian outback.

The healing he experienced was a wonderful miracle of God's grace, Tex was newly born again and sincere in his desire to learn all he could about God. Pastor Glazbrook and the people of the church were praying and believing for him and God graciously answered their prayers.

The Wonder and the Mystery of Divine Healing
Alison Chant

CHAPTER ELEVEN

FIVE RULES OF FAITH

This chapter is a sermon preached in Tasmania by my husband Ken and printed in the *Revivalist* magazine August 1973. It was around this time that he was writing the books – *Faith Dynamics* and *Throne Rights*. I'm sure this is why these books have helped so many to believe God for their own healing. They were written out of a tremendous wave of healing power from '63 -'78. In '78 we moved to Sydney to Vision Bible College, and from there we journeyed two years later to the USA.

Ken's unwavering faith in God's healing power was instrumental in inspiring me to join with him in believing God for our miracle sons. Sermons like this one would have been the faith foundation for the many healings which appear in chapter one of this book.

God Only Answers the Prayer of Faith.

The Lord Jesus Christ said, *"If you believe, you will receive whatever you ask for in prayer."* (Mt 21:22)

So we learn that prayer alone is not sufficient to bring us the answer to our need: we must pray the **prayer of faith**. It is not enough just to ask, we have to ask **believing**.

What is the prayer of faith? How can we ask in prayer, believing? To pray the prayer of faith, five things are essential.

1. You must believe that God is able.

Deep in your heart there must be an unwavering conviction that God is easily able to answer your prayer. And this conviction must be alive and vibrant! So many people say, "God can do anything!" but their words are cold and dispassionate, there is no responding tingle of faith in their inmost soul, no thrill of joy at the immense ability of our mighty God.

A graphic example of the Lord's requirement of faith in his ability to answer prayer is seen in his words to the two blind men: *"Do you believe that **I am able to do this**? Yes Lord, they replied."* Then he touched their eyes, and said, **according to your faith will it be done to you.** *And their sight was restored."* (Mt 9:27-30)

Notice also that Jesus was very particular in his question to the blind men. He said, *"Do you believe that I am able to do this?* **"This"** This particular thing! So many say, "All things are possible." But that is a very broad statement. What is more important is the personal challenge, "Is **this thing** possible." We often find that people, in times of abundance, will easily say that God can do anything; but when faced with a sudden great need their certainty begins to waver, the problem looms like a massive mountain, and they are not so sure that God can really help them.

So, every time we pray the Lord challenges us as he did the two blind men, "Do you really believe I am able to do this thing?" If we can confidently respond in our hearts, "Yes Lord!" then he will certainly say to us, as he did to them, *"According to your faith will it be done to you."*

2. You must believe that God will.

To be successful, all prayer must be made on the basis of God's absolute trustworthiness. It is probably useless for you to pray if you are in two minds as to whether the Lord will really answer your prayer. The Psalmist recognised this need for a united heart and an unwavering confidence in God's trustworthiness. He cried, *"Teach me your way, O Lord, and I will walk in your truth;* **give me an undivided heart, that I might fear your name."** (Ps 86:11)

And again the scripture tells us *"when we ask* **we must believe and not doubt."** (that is never doubting that God will answer). *"Because he who doubts is like a wave of the sea, blown, and tossed by the wind. That man should not think he will receive anything from the Lord."* (Ja 1:6-8)

Again we are told very plainly and bluntly, *"Without faith it is* **impossible** *to please God, because anyone who comes to him* **must believe that he exists and that he rewards those who earnestly seek him.** (He 11:6)

Faith in God is simply absolute trust or confidence in God, and the scripture says without such faith it is impossible for us to please God. This is quite reasonable. As a father, it would hurt me deeply if my son showed that he did not trust me, and had no confidence in my word. Yet God is vastly more reliable than any man. So Jesus said, *"If you, then, though you are evil, know how to give good gifts to your children,* **how much more will your Father in heaven give good gifts to those who ask him!"** (Mt 7:11)

Therefore we must break through all inward distrust if we would successfully pray. We can do this best by coming to God's own Word and taking hold of such promises as this: *"God is not a man, that he should lie, nor a son of man, that he should change his mind. Does he speak and then not act? Does he promise and not fulfil?"* (Nu 23:19)

Believe it then, **God will answer your prayer.**

3. *Believe that now is God's time to answer your prayer.*

Frequently people pray just on the off-chance that God might hear them and answer their prayer. Others are not quite so casual, but they still pray without any real expectancy that God will give them just what they ask for; they scarcely dare hope for any more than an approximate answer some time in the indefinite future. But we must learn that immediate expectation is just as important as prayer. **A settled belief that God heard and granted our request the moment we prayed is a vital requirement of successful prayer.**

Two scriptures press this truth upon us very firmly: Jesus said, *"Therefore I tell you, whatever you ask for in prayer, **believe that you have received it**, and it will be yours"* (Mk 11:24). So as soon as we pray, we must believe that our request is granted, and then we shall have what we asked for. The beloved disciple John expanded Jesus words, and wrote; *"This is the confidence we have in approaching God: that if we ask anything according to his will, he hears us. And if we know that he hears us – whatever we ask – **we know that we have** what we asked of him."* (1 Jn 5:14-15)

This then is the order in which we should pray:

From the Word we should find out what God wants to do for us; then we must ask for what we need; then we must believe that God listened to our prayer; then we must believe that he granted our request; then we must count ourselves as already being the owners of the thing we asked for; then we shall certainly have it!

People! No matter how impossible it may seem, **if you have God's promise on it, then pray with absolute assurance, believe with simple unshakeable trust, and know that God has answered your prayer. Believe without doubting, and in time the answer will appear!**

4. Believe in the power of your own prayer.

A great number of people satisfactorily observe all the principles we have mentioned; their faith in God, to all outward appearance is sure and confident, yet still they fail. Why? **It is often because their faith in God is not linked with faith in themselves.**

Let me explain that. We must realise that it is not possible to claim faith in one part of the scripture while rejecting another. If we want to believe what the Bible says about God and his promises, we must also believe what it says about us and our prayer.

Now, we so often hear people complaining: *"I am not worthy"*; *"God won't listen to my prayer"*; *"I have no faith" "I am too weak"*; *"The devil stops me from praying"*; *"I know the Lord can do it but will he really listen to my prayer";* and a host of other such-like defeated and anxious uncertainties. But into the teeth of these murmurings is hurled the emphatic declaration of God saying what you really are in Christ, and giving you open access into his grace and all his goodness.

Listen to these words, *"In him and through faith in him we may approach God with freedom and confidence."* (Ep 3:12), *"For through him we both have access to the Father."* (2:18), *"Let us then approach the throne of grace with confidence, so that we may receive mercy and find grace to help us in our time of need."* (He 4:16), *"Therefore, brothers, since we have confidence to enter the Most Holy Place by the blood of Jesus...**let us draw near to God with a sincere heart in full assurance of faith**...let us hold unswervingly to the hope we profess **for he who promised is faithful."*** (He 10:19-23)

People! Remember **your prayer has power if you will only believe in the power of your prayer!**

5. *Make your prayer an active one.*

Many prayers fail because they are too passive, they lack aggression, and the bold actions that result from real faith. Men and women of Bible days were people who prayed in real earnest; there was energy and passion and strength in their praying. The Lord Jesus Christ once said, *"...The kingdom of heaven has been forcefully advancing and **forceful men lay hold of it."*** (Mt 11:12)

Then again the Lord placed the emphasis on human command and action rather than merely asking God to do something, when he said, *"(you can)* **say to this mountain**, *move from here to there and it will move. Nothing will be impossible for you"* (Mt 17:20). And again, *"(you can)* **say to this mulberry tree, 'Be uprooted and planted in the sea, and it will obey you."** (Lu 17:6) References like these indicate that it is not enough to pray only. It is by prayer and waiting upon God and making our requests known to him that faith is strengthened in our hearts; we gain confidence, knowing that our request is granted. But having received that full assurance, it is then necessary to rise up in vigorous faith and claim the answer from heaven.

In fact, we should go even further, as Jesus said, and take hold of the authority we have in his name, and stand before the mountain that hinders us, and command it to be removed. You can boldly and forcefully charge the mountainous problems, or the deeply rooted trunk of sin and sickness, to be uprooted from your life, and cast into the ocean depths of God's deliverance.

Prayer gives you strength, courage and determination, so that your faith will become immovable. When such an immovable, irresistible faith strikes against the mountain of sickness or sin or bondage, the mountain must disintegrate.

Prayer will graft into your life the strong right arm of faith. But then you must act in authoritative command, maintaining a steadfast confidence that what you speak in faith will come to pass.

So, if you have a great need in your life, know that you can find the answer to it in the prayer of faith; believe that **God is able** to meet your need; believe that **God will meet** your need; believe that your prayer has power with God; believe that now, this very day, is God's day to hear you and grant your request; and rise up in bold faith, declaring that the work is done!

Jesus said, "**Ask, and you will receive, and your joy will be complete.**" (Jn 16:24)

CHAPTER TWELVE

A FINISHED WORK

The following testimony of healing is remarkable in that Dorothy Woolf is a nursing sister (now retired), and was for some years Matron of the Launceston General Hospital. Because of this she is well aware of the importance of proof and has provided it for us. She and her husband Ted were important members of our church when we were in Launceston and they are still dear friends. They remain busy in the Lord's work in Launceston. This testimony is a very recent one which Dorothy gave publicly in January 2006.

Healing From Systemic Lupus Erythematosis

When Jesus cried, *"It is finished"* (Jn 19:30) I believe that was not a cry of defeat but of victory. He had accomplished his purpose of completing everything his Father had for him to do. His mission was completed and that mission included healing for our physical body. (1Pe 2:24)

I now have faith in this healing work of Christ, but this has not always been the case. In times gone by I have given mental assent to it and said, "I know God heals." But, until now, I've never really known that he would heal me when I asked him to. There is a vast difference.

Things have changed over the last year and a half. My doctor thought I had Systemic Lupus

Erythematosis (S.L.E.), with kidney involvement. Blood and urine tests confirmed her suspicions.

A Specialists appointment was made for confirmation but I couldn't get in for four months. I believe this delay was divinely appointed as it gave me time to get serious about my faith in divine healing.

Devouring Scripture

I devoured healing and faith scriptures, wrote them out, confessed them, claimed them, prayed over them, studied them and did everything I could to build up my faith. The more I waited on God the more I realised that Jesus had already healed me. He had already done all he could to make me whole, it was now up to me to appropriate my healing by faith.

As far as I could see, James 5:14 was the only scripture specifically for sick Christians. So I was prayed for and while the prayer was being uttered I just knew in my heart I did not have lupus. So I came against the symptoms. I claimed the healing that was already mine. I knew it was done.

Why did I have these symptoms? Because I didn't really understand what faith was or what it entailed, but I learned as I waited on God.

This is what I learned:

Satan is the author of sin and sickness. Jesus defeated him at the cross. Through the blood of Jesus I am redeemed out of the hand of the enemy.

(Ps 107:2) Through the blood of Jesus the devil and his works have no place in me, and no power over me, because of all that Jesus did for me on the cross.

The Law of the Spirit of Life

We all live by either of two laws,

1. The law of earthly, natural things; that is the law of sin and death, or,

2. The law of the Spirit of life in Christ Jesus. (Ro 8:2)

The spiritual versus the natural; the truth of the word versus our feelings and emotions; revelation knowledge versus learned knowledge. It's our choice under which law we live.

We live under the law of the Spirit of life in Christ Jesus by faith. I had faith, I believed and trusted God, but I learned that there is more to this idea. I learned that I must walk by means of faith, not by means of external appearances (2 Co 5:7). I realized I had been living by what my five senses told me, what I could see, hear, touch, smell, or taste but now I had to learn to walk by faith.

God Requires Faith

I had always known that God could heal sickness, now I learned that he required faith from me.

We who are born again are new creations. Old things have passed away, and we are redeemed out of the hand of the enemy; translated out of the kingdom of darkness, into the kingdom of light. Everything belonging to the old sinful life stopped having the potential to affect us the moment we were born again. As we stand before the Father we are complete in him who is head over all power, authority, dominion and orders of satanic power. (Ep 1:19-23) We who are in Christ can stand absolutely complete in him. When we took him as our Saviour we passed out of the realm of darkness, sickness, death, sin and Satan's dominion into the realm of light and life as a member of the body of Christ.

Jesus bore our diseases on his body on the cross. So we are healed. Just as our sins were borne by him and they have been dealt with, forgotten by God (Ps 103:12), so it is with sickness and disease, they were borne for us on the cross. It is finished. Our spirits are alive to God, sickness and disease having lost their potential for dominion over us; they no longer have a right to reign over us in our bodies.

Jesus as our substitute was once made sick with our diseases. (1Pe 3:18) But no more, in God's mind we are cleansed of all sin, disease and sickness through our substitute.

My Decision

I had to decide what I would do in the face of these facts. I decided to say, *"I am what the word says I am."* That is a faith confession. When we believe that what God says is true, confess it and possess it, it becomes a reality to us. We are then acting on the Word of God and making the Word work for us.

I realised it was up to me. I had to have faith! We all have faith, it is a gift from God, but I had to learn to use it properly.

So I saturated myself in the scriptures, quoted them out loud, built my faith up and discovered through studying Dr Ken Chant's book *Faith Dynamics* that faith is rational, based on the integrity of the Word of God and the absolute trustworthiness of God himself.

Jesus is the author and finisher of my faith and I trust him implicitly. That is what faith is. It's not wishful thinking or hoping for something we have to pluck out of the air. Hope says, *"please"*, but faith says, *"thanks"*.

My Steps to Healing

Besides building up my faith I learned that there were other steps to appropriating my healing and they were:

1. Ask for a "rhema", a quickened word from the Bible, Romans 8:2, was my "rhema" word.

2. Be specific in prayer. I claimed my freedom from the symptoms of lupus.

3. Apply the promise verbally, "I w*ill trust the Lord, I will not be afraid or doubt, despite the symptoms. I know the truth and reality of the word of God are a higher law than the law of sin and death."*

4. Thank him for the finished work. *"Stand fast therefore in the liberty wherein Christ has set you free."* (Ga 5:1a) All this despite what your senses tell you.

I realized that when we know and act upon the knowledge of who we are and what we are in Christ we live as the new creations we already are spiritually.

My specialist's visit confirmed what I already knew...I didn't have lupus. So, I went back to my GP. She repeated the tests which are proof of the healing that had occurred in my body. Some tests were repeated at a later date as well.

A Copy of the Test Results.

Test Normal	1st visit	2nd visit	3rd visit
A,N,A, <80	160	80	-
CREATININE. 44-80	116	65	-
UREA <11.9	11.7	8.9	7.8
URIC ACID 0.34	0.45	0.27	0.27
H. B. 115-165	112	121	125
E. S. R. <20	24	21	20

I praise God for showing me the truth that set me free to realise that healing was already mine for the taking.

When Jesus said, *"It is finished"*. He meant it, *"He is not a man that he should lie."* (Nu 23:19a) *(Dorothy Woolf).*

Some of the scriptures Dorothy found most helpful:

Without faith it is impossible to please God. (He 11:6)

Faith comes by hearing and hearing by the Word of God. (Ro 10:17)

Attend to my words, incline your ear to my sayings, let them not depart from your eyes, keep them in the midst of your heart for they are life to those who find them and health to all their flesh. (Pr 4:20-22)

He sent his word and healed them. (Ps 107:20)

According to your faith be it unto you. (Mt 9:29)

As you have believed, so it will be done for you. (Mt 8:13)

All things, whatsoever you believe, when you ask in prayer, you shall receive. (Mt 21:22)

The prayer of faith will raise him up. (Ja 5:14)

If you can believe, all things are possible to him who believes. (Mk 9:23)

Your faith has made you whole. (Lu 8:48)

The Wonder and the Mystery of Divine Healing
Alison Chant

CHAPTER THIRTEEN

ALL THINGS ARE POSSIBLE!

To understand the background of the healing gift that has been seen in the ministry of Pastor Ken Tydeman and his wife Marjorie you must look into the preparation for that ministry that began long before the fruition.

Ken suffered great pain as a child with osteomyelitis in his right arm and left leg, his arm was in plaster for many months and his leg had to be operated on. He was not permitted to ride a bicycle until he was fourteen because of the danger of a recurrence of the disease should he have a fall. As a result of his own pain he has great compassion for the sick and suffering.

Ken became a Christian when, at the age of seventeen, he was arrested by the Holy Spirit while seated in the gutter with a drunken friend. He had just missed being hit by a car and had escaped serious injury.

"At 2.15 a. m. I realised that I could either die like a dog or be part of a future in the unknown," he said.

He decided this was no way to continue his life, gave his heart to the Lord, and sixteen hours later was preaching the gospel in a street meeting in Parramatta. In 1950 Ken spent fifty days in prayer and fasting with some friends, seeking for God to move in miracle- working power. During those fifty days they travelled together in a large van covered with scripture texts, and were invited to hold meetings in various country churches.

His wife Marjorie, whom he met in 1950 and married in July 1954, has been a partner in their healing ministry from the beginning. She has a miraculous healing testimony and because of this a great faith in the power of God to heal and deliver. She gave her testimony at a *Women's Aglow* meeting and graciously allowed me to transcribe it.

Marjorie's Testimony

> *"The steadfast love of the Lord never ceases, his mercies never come to an end; they are new every morning; great is thy faithfulness."* (Lamentations 3:22-23)

The Lord is the one who brings joy on top of joy! God's mercies never fail! They are new every day.

I was born with a blood disease. There was also an infection in my blood and the combination didn't work out very well, so many times I was sick. When I was about six and a half years of age I was dying in the local hospital with a tumour on the brain. I'd gone into a coma.

We belonged to a denomination that loved the Lord very much but they used to pray *"if it be thy will"* prayers. The elders would come and they would anoint me and they would pray, *"Lord if it be your will, heal Marge otherwise give her a safe entry into glory."*

That's Not Active Faith!

That's not faith! They prayed for me this way. I don't remember the prayer myself, but my mother often spoke about it. After I'd been in a coma for several days, my mother and father were beside my bed waiting for the dreadful moment when the end would come. My father was looking at the local newspaper and saw an advertisement, *"Jesus Christ, the same, yesterday today and forever."* It was for some special revival meetings. My father knew this was a verse of Scripture and that caused faith to rise in his heart, so immediately he spoke to my mother about this verse of Scripture.

The advertisement went on to say, *"Come, bring the halt, the lame, the deaf, and the blind."* That's how they advertised back then. Prayer would be given for these people. My father went down to the picture theatre where the meetings were being held and asked the preacher to pray for me. He also asked him to come to the hospital and pray. It was time then for the meeting to start so the preacher said, *"I'll pray now and things will be alright."* How's that for faith!

He prayed there on the steps of the building and as part of his prayer he spoke in tongues. My father had never heard anyone speak in tongues before. They used to say speaking in tongues was of the devil, but with it came the blessing and the peace of God so my father knew speaking in tongues was not of the devil. With it came faith into his heart. He came back to the hospital and he said to mum, the preacher prayed for Margy and things are going to be alright. He'll come up after the meeting and pray.

Healed at Death's Door

I was there in a coma. Different ones had been talking around my bedside. I could hear and understand what they were saying, and I was in darkness and a fear that I'll never forget, it was so terrible. As I lay there in this coma I was conscious that someone came and stood by my bedside. To me it was as though Jesus came, I didn't know much about Jesus, but it was as though he came and stood by my bed. How wonderful to know when Jesus is there. And the preacher, Fred Van Eyk, prayed and after he prayed he shouted, *"The work is done, hallelujah."*

My bed was in the middle of a large ward of ladies, by the sister's desk. I heard the words, the whole hospital heard them! I came out of the coma to hear those words echoing up and down the hospital.

They didn't release me from hospital immediately. I was healed of the tumour on the brain at that particular moment of time but the doctors kept me for observation for twenty four hours, and then I was released. However, I was not healed of the blood disease at that time, though I was healed of the tumour on the brain.

Parents Asked to Repudiate Healing

We went back to our local church on the Sunday and word had got around that Pentecostals had prayed for Margy. My parents were brought to the front of the meeting and were asked to say that the man who had prayed for me was of the devil, and that they would have nothing more to do with him. My father thought for a few moments and then he said, *"The preacher prayed in the name of Jesus and Margy is here to tell the story so we can't say that!"*

With those words they marched us down the aisle of the church, they shook the dust off the mat at the door and they asked us not to come back any more unless we changed our minds. To me, as I look back, that was not a sad day, but a happy day of deliverance, because we needed to know all about Jesus, we needed to know every part of the scripture from cover to cover and not explain any of it away. We needed to know Jesus and would only know him by knowing his Word.

From then on we went to a Pentecostal church and I grew up in a Pentecostal church where the power of God was manifested in those early days. As the years came and went I still suffered with this blood condition which caused cancers to happen. I cannot fill you in on all of the occasions that I suffered but I praise God that I was in a church that prayed for me and there were those in the church that prayed and prayed and prayed again. Once again the hour was close when I should have died, medically speaking, but Jesus interfered again! He is the answer.

Another Tumour in My Throat

This time I had a tumour in the throat area, and the roots of the cancer had gone all around the voice box part of my throat, affecting it. I was in the hospital because of this condition and the doctors decided to cut open my throat and put in place some tubes so they could let a bit of moisture go down, and so on, to relieve the problem. The doctor stepped aside for a few moments, as he explained later, and while he stepped aside to pick up something the tumour started to release from my body. It oozed out of the hole they had made in my throat for the tubes.

This was the same doctor we had for all my illnesses, and he caught this tumour on a tray and there it was. I was healed of that tumour at that time. The doctor ran down the corridor of the hospital, shouting, *"You have done it again, you have done it again."*

My mother recognized his voice and she thought, *"What is wrong this time. Why is he carrying on?"* The doctor came into the waiting room with this horrible specimen on the tray for my mother to have a look at. He knew that Jesus had done it again!

A Period of Disobedience

At this stage I had grown old enough to say that I appreciated the Lord, I often testified of his power, I often told of his grace when I was asked to. But it

is one thing to appreciate Jesus and it's another thing to say, *"Jesus, I'll serve you."*

As a young teenager I appreciated the Lord very much, deep down in my heart, but I was not prepared to serve him. So I got to the point where mum would say to get ready for church and I would grumble that I didn't want to go. My father would say, *"She is old enough to choose for herself, let her go."*

Praise God for a scheming mother that brought me, and brought me, and brought me to church. This particular day we were having a visitor in our church and my mother wanted me to go because the cancer was healed from my body, but my voice was still affected, and my hearing was affected. One ear was deaf and the other was partly deaf, so if you wanted to talk to me you had to shout on the right side before I would catch on to what you were saying.

That Sunday morning the meeting started with singing and praying for those needing healing and then it was time for communion. The preacher called for those needing healing before he preached. He didn't know anything about me or my family. He prayed for me and immediately I heard everything clearly. The sermon that followed was based on the verse, *"Go and sin no more lest a worse thing come upon thee."*

Addicted to Morphine

I squirmed, as I'd been addicted to morphine from the age of ten; it was a horror all of its own. There are other drugs for pain these days, but then I was addicted to morphine because that was all they had to dull the pain of the cancers one after the other.

This was another sickness all on its own. As I sat there I thought to myself I had ached more than anyone else, I was sick more than anyone else, *"Lord how could it be any worse? How could my life be any worse than it is?"* And I sat there and squirmed some more. I was under conviction. The meeting came to an end and they closed it with prayer and I left before any one could say the message was for me. I knew that Jesus had spoken to my heart, I knew that Jesus was real and I had resisted him, so as the days came and went that "worse thing" did happen to me.

A Terrible Accident

My father had several Chevrolet cars, he had one jacked up on bricks in a shed for spare parts, the wheels were missing from it and the car was about knee high off the floor of the shed. There were "chooks" camped all over the car and this particular day my father and mother decided to do something with the shed and they were going to tow this particular car out and turn the shed into a garage. However, I was there before dad had even put a chain or a rope or anything onto the car, I was there standing beside it making a noise to shoo the "chooks" out of the shed.

For some unknown reason, (we had played on that car many times yet it had never fallen), that particular day it fell. The wooden running boards that went along the old chevrolet cars were missing but the steel supports were stuck out the side that usually held up the wood. One of those steel pieces was sticking out right at the back of my leg as it fell. It hit one leg half way down and it sliced right through to the bone and right down to the foot. The other leg it went half way through to the bone and dragged all the way down to the foot.

I had this incurable blood disease, I wasn't supposed to be knocked, I couldn't run and play games like other young people. I had never played a game. I couldn't knock myself on a door knob, if I bruised myself slightly I would get another cancer. And so here I was with this terrible accident that had happened to my leg. My mother held the skin on top of the worst leg while they raced me to hospital to try and do something about it. The doctor gave me no hope, he said to my mother, *"We will have to amputate the worst leg first, that's for sure. We'll see about the other one."*

My Mother Cultivated a Vision

But when the hours were very dark and my mother was very desperate with the Lord; on some of those occasions when it seemed like I would die she cultivated a vision. She believed in what the scripture said, and the scripture says, *"Without a vision the people perish."* She cultivated a vision of me preaching the gospel on the back of a semi trailer truck, when there were no semi trailer trucks, like the one she could see, in Australia. She had seen pictures of them in America and so she cultivated a vision of me preaching on the streets of Manly on the back of a semi trailer truck. What a vision!

It was almost impossible to believe it could come to pass back then. When the darkest hours would come my mother would say to the Lord, *"I'll see it happen!"*

"She Will Live in Jesus Name!"

It was a faith thing for her and when it seemed impossible she would say, *"She will live in Jesus name"!*

One time I came out of a coma with my mother standing at my pillow and she was pointing her finger at me saying, *"You will live in Jesus name"!* And live I did! Praise God.

However, here I was now in hospital with these leg problems. As the days proceeded gangrene set in and the doctor met my mother one morning and he said to her, *"We'll have to amputate the worst leg first, I want you to sign the form for the surgery."*

My mother thought of her vision and she thought to herself, *"In my vision she wasn't legless."* So she said to the doctor, *"We'll wait one more day."* That day proceeded and a couple of days went by and the doctor met mum again on another morning and he said, *"It's too late now for both legs, we'll have to act today."*

Now the doctor had done his rounds the night before and my mother said her God didn't fail and so she was scheming another scheme even though she knew it was impossible this thing should happen, so she said to the doctor, *"Have you seen Margie this morning?"*

She knew very well he'd done his rounds the night before and was ready for the morning surgery, but as the doctor insisted on surgery to my mother she said, *"We'll go down and see her now and then I'll sign the form."*

Gangrene Healed

My mother had those few extra minutes up her sleeve. She knew somehow God was going to heal the gangrene. As they came down and uncovered my legs every trace of gangrene and unhealthy flesh had disappeared and the legs seemed quite healthy and they smelled very good. Hallelujah! Isn't God good, isn't his mercy wonderful!

From that time onwards they began to try to put skin around the wounds on my legs. They took skin grafts from all over my body. That didn't work very well so eventually they pulled the skin right around my legs and they were very ugly I tell you. One leg had no muscle to walk with and the other leg had a little bit more. From the time that the gangrene subsided until the time I was discharged from hospital was fourteen months. In that fourteen months I had grown some so the leg that was the worst damaged became four and three quarter inches shorter than the other one. When I was discharged from hospital I had to learn to walk on a boot that had steel prongs with a false heel on it and a walking stick and a crutch. To help me to walk someone would have kick my boot at the back, that leg would come forward and then I could bring the other one around and forward. And that's the way it had to be, medically there was nothing more that the doctors could do. There were still a couple of marks on my legs that hadn't healed. On one leg in particular the scars looked like zippers gone wrong. They were horrible. Now it was time for me to go back to the doctor and get the medicine I needed and it was a couple of days after I'd been discharged that I was to go to the doctor's rooms.

Just near the doctor there was a fashionable store that my mother and I passed and there were all the pretty things that were coming up for Easter time spread out in the window looking really lovely.

I'd been in hospital for a long time and I'd been out of circulation. I didn't know the latest fashions and there were all those beautiful things to be looked at. My mother began scheming again. She wanted me to go to the Easter convention with her and I said, *"No way."* I knew if I went to the Easter convention it meant going to the city and I would have to be there Good Friday morning, afternoon and evening and also for three meetings on Sunday. I wasn't going to be in that, no way.

As I was looking in the shop window at all the pretty things my mother thought, *"Aha, maybe this will get her to the meetings."*

There was this beautiful pink frock with little tiny pleats all the way around it, they looked so pretty and mum said to me, *"I'll buy you that frock if you'll come to the Easter Convention with me."*

Well, you might think that was scheming, but I'd never had a new frock from a shop before. My mother had always sewed and altered things for us and we always looked pretty good, but I'd never had a brand new frock. My parents couldn't afford them because they had medical bills after medical bills and hospital bills after hospital bills to pay over the years of my illnesses, but here mum was saying to me, *"I'll buy you that frock if you'll come to the Easter Convention.*

God Was Behind My Decision

This made me realise how much mum wanted to take me to the Easter Convention. So on the way home I was churning inside myself, thinking things over and I guess God was also putting his thumb on my decision as well. So on the way home I decided to tell mum, *"You needn't buy me that frock, but I'll go to the Easter Convention with you on one condition."*

She said, *"What's that."* I said, *"I'll go to make you happy, for no other reason, I'll just go to make you smile but I'll turn off, I won't hear a word."*

Well, my mother didn't mind that. We went home and she went back and bought me that frock after all. I went off to the Convention thinking I was the best dressed there, the pink dress was so pretty, and I loved it, and I loved mum all the more. Mum was a wonderful mum.

We went to the first service of the Easter Convention and I turned off my mind very well and was pleased with myself. In the afternoon service there was a missionary there from India. The Lord does tell preachers what to say most of the time, and this lady from India began to preach on the Second Coming of the Lord Jesus. Well, I couldn't turn this off, I had to listen because I had a grandmother who was an artist and she had purchased for me a wonderful picture of the Lord coming in the clouds of glory. I had this on my wall at home and so I listened to every word the preacher had to say. As she started to come toward the end of the message, she said, *"I know the Lord is going to come real soon, he has to come quickly because scripture says two are going to be grinding at the mill, one will be taken and the other left. India is one of the most underprivileged countries of the world and they are bringing in machinery to do the grinding. So the Lord has to come soon or he won't find two people grinding at the mill."*

I started to get a little scared, down in my heart that churning started, *"I've got to get out of this place, I've got to run."*

But I couldn't make an excuse to go outside on my own, because I couldn't go out on my own! I needed my mother or my aunt to kick my foot. I wasn't game to try to get out on my own with a crutch and a walking stick, so I sat there.

My Struggles With God

The service came to an end and we were having tea together in the big hall and everyone was talking when word got around the table that the preacher who was booked to preach that night couldn't make it. They announced that the same preacher who preached in our local assembly, *"Go, sin no more lest a worse thing come upon thee,"* just before my accident, had been chosen to preach.

I thought, *"Oh! no way, I can't hear this man, I can't listen to what he has to say."* So I started on my mother and my aunt and raised every excuse that I could think of. That I'd been sitting too long, I was tired, they needed to take me home. But, do you know what my mother said? *"We've come for the whole loaf."* She wanted to hear all of the sermons for the day!

I thought of something else; I've seen this happen many times. When the power of God starts to move across a congregation there are always those who don't want to be part of the move of God, or to sit under his glory. There are always those who wriggle a bit, they don't want to be touched by the Lord, and so they use an excuse to go out to the bathroom. So I thought, *"This will do, when the preacher gets up and announces his word, I'll tell mum she has to take me out to the bathroom."*

But my mother and my aunt were a bit cleverer than me, and the Lord was a little bit faster than all of us put together. When it came time for me to use my excuse I realized there were five people each side of us and there was no way for me to get out without asking at least five people to leave their seats so I could get out. I wasn't brave enough! It would have disturbed everyone as the floor was wooden without a carpet to soften the sound of footsteps.

There I sat and the more I tried to turn off the more I heard, the more I tried to think of all sorts of other things the more I listened. I thought, *"My mother has been talking to this guy about me; she's told him all about me."*

The preacher was preaching away with great fire, and I was churning up and trying to throw the words away. The faster I tried to get rid of what he was saying the more it came. I nudged my mother and accused her of talking to this guy about me. She said, *"No, I haven't, I haven't spoken to him."*

Jesus Speaks to Me Through the Sermon

I knew my mother told the truth, she didn't lie and so I realised, *"This must be Jesus speaking to me."* God has a wonderful way of letting us know that he is real and that he speaks. I knew this was Jesus and so I had to listen. As I listened I started to make all kinds of decisions in my mind and in my heart, though I made excuses for myself as well as decisions. As the meeting came to a close I yielded,

"Yes Lord, I'll serve you."

As I made that decision a peace came over my heart and my life. The pastor made an appeal for people to come forward, but I had already said to the Lord, *"I'll give my life to you when I go home to bed tonight."*

I didn't want to drag myself out to the front because of the embarrassment. With that decision made there was a peace and joy that came over me. Then, as the appeal was being made, the people began singing, *"All to Jesus I surrender, all to him I freely give."*

I said, *"Jesus you've got me in a corner, I can't run. Why am I going to give my life to you?"* I thought of all the things of the world that I would like to experience and I entered into conflict for a moment. I needed to sort out the vital question, *"Do I surrender all to Jesus? Do I freely give him all?"*

I Finally Give in to God

The service was coming to an end, the pastors were praying for the people out front, and then they were going back to their seats. They called on someone to close in prayer, and then another pastor got up from the back of the platform and he came forward and said, *"Just a minute, there's one person out there who didn't respond, there's one person who didn't come."*

I knew it was me, and then someone else came out to the front and I thought, *"I'm saved."* This happened three times, three times that man said, *"The person hasn't yet come tonight."* I knew by this time it was really me, that if I didn't go forward that man would keep asking, four times, five times and even more so I made plans to move to the front.

Looking back I remembered times in the night when, because of the morphine addiction, I would wake up screaming and my dad would sing me back to sleep singing the hymn, *"There's power in the blood."* I would go to sleep to that song. One night I was in such a terror, I felt the devil was all around the room, all the things in my room terrified me, in the darkness it seemed they were all devils. I tried to get under the mattress away from the devils and I couldn't hide from them. That particular night I decided to look out the window because somewhere out there I thought surely the Lord must be.

Jesus Promises me Joy and Peace

It doesn't matter how many times we have said, *"No"*, to the Lord, it doesn't matter how many times we've excused ourselves, if we will draw near to him he will draw near to us. I looked out the window, looking for Jesus because I was in such misery and torment. And it was as if all the heavens opened, and there was the wonderful heavenly choir singing in harmony all the praise of heaven. It was just beautiful, and in the middle of it Jesus came and spoke to me, and he said, *"If you serve me I'll heal you completely."* He told me a few personal things, that I won't repeat, but amongst them he said, *"I'll give you joy, I'll give you joy, I'll give you peace."* These were the two things I didn't have, I didn't have joy and peace.

So now I was in the church, getting ready stand to my feet, and I thought, *"There is my vision Lord, I'll have joy first of all thank you very much."*

Jesus Sets Me free from Morphine Addiction

As I stood to my feet all nervousness left me, before that moment I was scared to walk to the front for I had to have either my mother or my aunt to help me out and there was the noise of my boot on the floor to think of. Now, however, the joy of the Lord became my portion. I began to laugh, and I laughed and I laughed and I laughed. All nervousness and embarrassment left me. It didn't matter anymore who was there, I was just coming to the front with the joy of the Lord. I had to wait for five people to get out of their seats for me to come forward, but at the same time I stood tall, I just knew, that I knew, that I knew that I was brought out from the effect of morphine, I knew I was set free, I was loosed, my mind was clear, I wasn't like a tree swinging in the breeze any more. Jesus had set me free and he'd given me his joy. It is joy unspeakable and full of glory and you can't explain how real it is. When Jesus blesses you with real joy it doesn't go away, it is always there. It is well over forty years since that joy came in the storm and in the darkest night. There's joy, Jesus gave me his joy.

That night as I came to the front the pastors prayed over a laughing sinner. Usually you pray over a crying sinner. They prayed over a laughing sinner, and I laughed all the way home. On the way home, on the last Manly ferry for the night, there were many people, some of them were intoxicated and noisy, and there was me. I couldn't stop laughing and my mother kept saying, *"Ssh! Think where you are."*

I would be quiet for a few seconds and then I would start laughing and singing, because I knew that Jesus had set me free. Jesus said he would make me whole, Jesus said he would heal me all over, I was laughing and reveling in the wonder of seeing myself whole. I could see myself playing football with my brothers, I could see myself running and doing things I hadn't done before, and the joy and the blessing of thanking Jesus for my healing was so real. I went home that night just thanking and praising God because he had set me free. I had no way of telling if my blood condition had gone or not, but I knew Jesus said he would heal me and that was good enough for me. I got home, I took my boot off and put my things on the dressing table and went to bed that night for the very first time without all the medicine I used to take, and I slept. Oh! the bed was beautiful, for the first time. I had always been scared of my room, I thought my room was full of devils but now the blessing of the Lord was upon it and it was beautiful.

My Leg Grows and I Rise Up and Walk

The next morning I rose from my bed and walked through the house as if nothing had happened. At the table my father gave me this weird look up and down. With that weird look it registered, I looked down and I had two legs the same length. The one that was four and three quarters of an inch shorter had grown over night. I had a little muscle on the leg that had no muscle, it was enough to walk on, enough to run on. I tell you I ran and I walked all day. I took a run and a jump into a great big pile of grass where my father had weeded the garden the day before and the grass felt nice. I hadn't run, I hadn't played, I didn't know what it was to play sport. Now I was set free, can you imagine how I felt? By the next morning, the second morning, when I got up the two holes that hadn't healed properly were healed, the scars that looked like zippers had smoothed down, the big bubbles had disappeared. I've just a couple of scars and one dent now and it is a wonderful testimony to the glory of God. He didn't leave me ugly, he didn't leave my legs a sight to behold, he made them pretty legs to preach the gospel on because Jesus is real and he does all things well. He doesn't half do a job, he does it well, he does it thoroughly.

This healing began with my promise to surrender all to Jesus. I promised the Lord that I would serve him seven days a week and twenty four hours a day. I had seen some Christians who could put on an act on Sunday and look good and then go out and say all manner of evil things outside the church. When you are unsaved you pick on those kinds of people. I knew that wasn't the way, it had to be, *"All to Jesus I surrender."* We need a full walk, an honest walk with Jesus. Jesus sees the heart and he knows what is on the inside, and he knows our endeavours, he knows if we try to walk with him. Even if we fall he will still bless us.

No More Blood Disease – I Am Completely Whole

From that day to this I've never had a cancerous growth on my body, and I never will. My blood disease was healed! Before I was healed I couldn't bump myself on a doorknob without getting a cancer. Now I did more than most young people. I was always running and jumping and playing. Once I was running for the ferry to go to work and I jumped onto the gangway only to find the railing I had meant to grab hold of was missing. I went into the water and they had to fish me out; indeed the ferry almost crushed me against the jetty but I wasn't even bruised, because now Jesus was with me, he was looking after me, I was his child.

Of course I had to stay behind, I was too wet to go to work, and then I realized my purse was still in the water with my whole week's pay in it so I dived in again to get my purse! Then I went home to change. We have a wonderful Lord and he has a sense of humour too!

The joy of the Lord is our strength and as we walk with him Christian life doesn't become a nightmare; it doesn't become a long drawn out sad life. The joy of the Lord is there because it is his divine joy, it is his divine life, it is his power, it is his glory that moves in us and around us and causes us to walk in him. Outside of that glory it is hard, but let us receive his glory, receive him afresh every day. *His mercies are new every morning. Great is his faithfulness.*

What a marvellous background for a healing ministry!

Ken Tydeman started out preaching the healing power of God in the early '50's in Manly and Marjorie came along to help after work each day. They have not stopped since. After twenty years as pastors in the Four Square Gospel Church in the city of Orange, New South Wales they were released into an itinerant healing ministry. They have held four tent campaigns over the years and have been travelling and preaching for the Lord in Australia, New Zealand, New Guinea and the USA.

Their healing ministry was reported in the *Penrith City Star,* Tuesday January 13th, 1987.

Do Miracles Happen? Tydeman's say, "Yes"

Travelling evangelists, Ken and Marjorie Tydeman, have devoted their lives to the preaching of the gospel and the revealing of miracles.

The Blaxland couple...are renowned for their ministry of healing. The Tydemans firmly believe in the power of God to perform miracles and claim to have seen many miraculous events take place during more than thirty years of ministry. Pastor Tydeman has tape recordings of personal testimonies from people who have walked away from his services completely healed of heart conditions, blindness, deafness, sickness and crippling diseases.

"It is a real witness for a non-believer to see a miracle happening right in front of his eyes," he

said.

"Marjorie and I have seen hundreds of people give their lives to Christ as a result of this. At one of our meetings we prayed for a woman who had been blind in one eye for four years. She received instant healing and her heart was full of praise for God. She was running around the church yelling and screaming. 'I can see, I can see!'"

At another service we witnessed the healing of an eleven year old boy who had suffered from a foot and muscle disorder since birth. When this boy came forward for healing his left foot was turned in at a forty five degree angle, he had a huge lump on his ankle and had (webbed) toes like those on a duck. There was no muscle behind his shin bone. After I prayed for him the congregation watched as this boy's leg grew half an inch, his foot straightened, his toes parted and the lump in his ankle disappeared. It was truly a miracle of God. Michael took half a day off school the following morning and went shopping to buy his first pair of normal shoes."

The Tydemans have travelled around Australia, America, New Guinea and New Zealand. They claim to have witnessed many kinds of miracles including the straightening of crossed eyes, the disappearance of skin blemishes and the growth of legs. They've seen the transformation of drug addicts and have always followed up the people who received healing at their meetings...

In our next chapter we have some of the exciting testimonies Ken and Marjorie have kept a record of during the last fifty six years.

The Wonder and the Mystery of Divine Healing
Alison Chant

CHAPTER FOURTEEN

GOD IS GOOD

The following testimonies come from the records kept by the Tydemans over the years. Some were recorded in local newspapers, some came in letter form from grateful people and some stories were recorded on tape at various times by various people who had received healing.

Thora Stands Up to Be Counted

This testimony concerning Mrs Thora Murray appeared in the *Blacktown City Star* Wednesday October 21st, 1987.

> Thora Murray has been walking tall since she was healed by evangelists Ken and Marjorie Tydeman in Blacktown early this year.
>
> Thora told the *Star* she was cured of a double curvature of the spine suffered since birth, a short right leg which "miraculously" grew and an arthritic hand which had forced her to abandon her lifetime hobby of painting.
>
> *"I read in the Penrith City Star (13th January '87) that the Tydemans were going to be holding a healing meeting at Blacktown and although I've never been a great church goer I felt somehow God was going to help me,"* she said.
>
> *"It had never entered my head to visit a healer before and it has completely changed my life. Since then I have been baptised and at my baptism I*

> *spoke in tongues and felt like I was going to rise out of the water. Since a child my back problem meant I had always been unable to do certain things although I've led a normal busy life. Growing up I couldn't run around like other kids and although I had surgery, nothing helped."*

She described her healing experience...

> *"I felt a warmth go through me and my leg grew and my spine straightened – it was like something was enfolding me,"* she said. *"I also later realised my rheumatism had disappeared and I could paint again."*

> *"I'm not a healer...I'm just a Christian messenger and have faith in God,"* said Ken Tydeman.

Obviously the reporter did her best to report this wonderful healing, though she was without a full understanding that it is Jesus who heals. Ken made sure that the article ended with a resounding declaration to this effect!

Thora is now ninety two years of age and still moving freely, Ken and Marjorie visit her regularly as Thora and her husband are their near neighbours in Blaxland, New South Wales.

Set Free From Mental Illness

Pastor Ken Tydeman and his wife prayed for Beryl, now Mrs Beryl Jackson, when she was a patient at Bloomfield Mental hospital. It was all they could do to get her to smile so great was the oppression that bound her.

Now today she is a happy wife and mother completely healed and a constant picture of joy. Praise God she no longer needs the glasses or the shock treatments. Christ has set her free!

The Tydemans signed her out of hospital and she remained with them for several years, healed by God's power.

On Saturday the 8th April 2000 Beryl, and her husband, Ray, celebrated their 40th wedding anniversary. They were married in the Four Square Gospel Church on April 8th 1960 and lived in the Orange district during their married life.

Beryl and Ray have five children and thirteen grandchildren and they are still joy filled!

June can Sing Again

This taped interview testimony concerning June Olsen was held in Orange, New South Wales. Now in her seventies, June recently became the wife of Dr Charles Taylor.

June had eighteen months in a mental hospital with conventional shock treatment, and also insulin shock which nearly killed her. This was then discontinued. She took many tablets as well as the shock treatment without gaining the help she needed. She finally came to the service, after some weeks of invitation, in her dressing gown and slippers. There she accepted the Lord as her Saviour and felt his great love and a wonderful peace.

As well as the mental problem she had been a trained singer, but her condition prevented her from being able to sing. After prayer she was invited to sing and she sang a verse and chorus of the Holy City. Her vocal cords were totally free. This encouraged her faith to believe for total healing so that a week later she gradually discontinued her tablets and finally threw the remainder down the drain. She had such peace and joy in her heart she no longer needed the drugs.

Her first husband was away shearing at the time of her healing, and when he came home and saw her so radiant with her face shining, he thought she must have another man in her life. He knew something had happened!

"I told him, yes I do have someone! I have Jesus Christ in my life," enthused June.

Now June takes her guitar and sings at nursing homes with a group of Christians. She sees the faces of the elderly light up as they enjoy the songs and the fellowship.

The next interview and the several interviews that follow were all recorded on tape with Ken Tydeman's help.

Myelin Sheath Restored to Nerve

I was prayed for sixteen years ago while I was living in Taree. In 1981 I was wrestling with my son, and sustained a severe neck injury. Since then I have been unable to raise my arms above my shoulder and I've been in severe pain. I went along to a church meeting in Taree on the October long weekend in 1983, and I was prayed for Wednesday night but felt no better. I went back on Thursday night and was prayed for again, this time by Marjorie Tydeman. My neck was in a cast at this time. The specialist had explained to me that the X-rays and Ct. scans had shown that the myelin sheath of the nerve in my spine supplying my upper limbs was crushed, and there was no possible way this could be corrected. Surgery was scheduled to be performed the next Tuesday at the Newcastle Hospital.

I knew something happened to me when Marjorie prayed for me. I felt warmth all the way down my back from my head, and I was able to raise my arms above my head for the first time in two years. I was also completely free of pain. After praying about the surgery, due to be performed the next Tuesday, I felt it right to continue with the operation. When the neuro-surgeon opened me up she was astounded to find the myelin sheath of the nerve in my spine completely restored, and this, she told me, she could not have done.

However, she went ahead with the spinal fusion she had planned and I was due to be in hospital for three weeks, but I was in only seven days. I was told I would need a brace for six months, but only had to wear it for two months and have never had to wear it since. I have no more pain and I'm still praising the Lord for what he did for me. Jesus healed me! *(Geoff Leonard)*

Allergies Healed

Around 1977 I was struck down, with an allergy. The swelling in my face, tongue and lips was three times normal size, the skin stretched so far it was painful. I wouldn't go outside at all so disfiguring was this condition, so I hardly worked at all. My doctor sent me to an immunologist who finally discovered I was allergic to twenty six different kinds of food. I was allergic to things like food additives, preservatives and natural products such as dairy products, chicken products, and wheat. The only fruit I could eat was pears which I grew to loathe. I ate things like fresh lamb chops, or cornflakes with pear juice instead of milk for breakfast, there were so few things I could eat. Finally the specialist found there were seven or eight foods which caused the swelling. Even though I was careful to avoid these foods the swelling gradually became worse, until finally I was not free for even one day at a time. This was disheartening but I tried to get on with my life. In 1983 my wife and I decided to go to Taree to visit friends. While we were there the friends invited me to a church service where Pastor Ken and Marjorie Tydeman were speaking on healing. I had been prayed for before with no result, but I felt this time was different, that God was going to do something for me. After the service I didn't feel any different but I acted out my faith by eating what everyone else was eating at supper time (apple pie and ice-cream). The result was I woke next morning totally healed after six years of suffering. (*Ken Pavey*)

Clubbed Feet Straightened

I had two children born with clubbed feet, one little girl is two and a half and a boy seven months old, both had clubbed feet. The children weren't in the meeting but prayers were said for their feet to be straightened. After we prayed for them I went home and the next morning when I dressed the little baby his feet had been straightened by the power of God and my daughter's feet were healed as well. Their feet are now perfect, there are only lines, the lines showing where the feet were twisted. God has healed them. *(Michelle Murray)*

Arthritis Healed

This testimony is from an interview with Mrs Goolagong, mother of Yvonne Goologong the tennis star.

I had arthritis and was in a bad condition. After climbing the stairs I would sit and cry because it was hurting so much. My sons told me of the healing meetings and when I arrived I needed help to get up the stairs into the church. When I came out for prayer, I was praying to God also. I saw a shining light and felt a burning feeling in my hips, right down to my knees. After prayer I moved quite freely. That night I went down the stairs of the church with no trouble and went home and slept well for the first time for a long time. Since then I have gone gold fossicking and walked over the rough ground with no trouble at all. I have been able to get into the van which has a high step and have played basketball with my grandchildren. People who saw me before couldn't believe it when they saw me playing. One of my legs was also shorter than the other before Mrs Tydeman prayed. While she was praying I could feel something happening, my bones were being rearranged and now I have no more trouble. *(Mrs Goologong)*

Curvature of the Spine Straightened

I am Bernie Fraser, 65 years of age, I had a curvature of the spine from when I was four years old and I lived with a frame for about three years. I was in hospital a total of five years as a boy and I was told in the early stages that I would possibly never walk again. I only had six years schooling because of the length of my stay in hospital. I had this curvature of the spine and it was like a question mark with a curve coming out at the back also which necessarily stunted my growth.

On Sunday night I went out for prayer. Brother Ken prayed for me and I felt a tensing of the muscles in my back and I seemed to get taller. My wife was standing beside me, and she felt my back and said, *"It's gone."*

Since that time I've been praising and rejoicing in the Lord because I've had a strange feeling in the muscles in my back, almost like a back ache, but I'm straight and at a conservative estimate my wife says I've grown at least an inch to an inch and a half. I'll be able to look down on her now! Praise the Lord. *(Bernie Fraser)*

Healed After Three Back Surgeries

This interview testimony was given on tape in Vidalia, Georgia USA, on Friday night November 1982. It concerns a healing gained through prayer three years previously.

In 1976 I had back surgery and was hospitalised from 12th March to 5th June. In '79 I had surgery in May and in the latter part of July I had surgery again. After the third surgery the neuro- surgeon said he could nothing more for me.

"You will be able to take care of your personal needs, but nothing else," he advised.

But somehow I felt that I couldn't live like that so I had my gun cleaned, I was ready to commit suicide. All I was waiting for was the place for this to happen. I was on so much medication, I was taking eight to ten muscle relaxants a day, three valium, fifty miligrams per day, two oevils, twenty five miligrams per day, and I was taking fifty miligrams of perpedan every three to four hours. I was not supposed to drive, I couldn't do anything. I thought to myself, what was the use of living; what was life worth to me? I didn't know God as my Saviour, I had previously taught a Methodist Sunday School class, but I was not a born again Christian.

So I had plans to commit suicide, but God sent a perfect stranger into my home to tell me about this Christian Fellowship and somehow I had the urge to come. I felt like I had to come. I was not supposed to drive. My sister in law doesn't drive but she came with me. I drove here, and I came into the service and after brother Tydeman ministered the Word of God I forgot about the physical needs that I had come for. I was thinking about my spiritual needs. My spirit needed healing and God miraculously saved me. He gave me a new life and also healed my back.

Today I hold down a full time job, I clean my house, I do all my outside yard work. I drive, I take no medication now, I have not taken one muscle relaxant, not one tranquilizer, not one valium, though I have taken a few perpedan. Now, for the last three years I have had to take no medication at all. I was healed November 30th 1979 at 9.20pm. Today my husband is saved, he is a born again Christian and is seeking the baptism of the Holy Spirit. We know that God is able! (*Lois Waring*)

Learning to Walk Again

The following testimony from Alan Jones was given fourteen months after his dramatic healing through prayer. Alan was well known in the district and had been featured in the local paper. Because of this many people knew of his condition. He was much liked and those who

knew Alan well, and the fact that he had been crippled for so long, were amazed by his healing. In 1994, after being unable to walk without crutches for fifteen years, with most of his time being spent in a wheel chair, Alan was instantly healed in one of Ken and Marjorie's meetings. Here is the extract from a local *Cumberland Newspaper*, April 1989:

"Despite being confined to a wheel chair, Alan has made the long and tiring journey from East Gosford to visit Mary, his wife, at Wyong Nursing Home three or more times a week, since she suffered a stroke last year. His day begins with a bus trip from East Gosford to the Gosford station where he boards a train for Wyong...John (Moore) handed over the new set of wheels (a Ventura Trike) to Alan on the Bert Newton Show last Thursday."

Alan came to the service to be prayed for, walking with the help of his crutches. He was unable to walk freely as he had been hit on the back of the neck with a rubber hose as a child. Because of this the condition of his spine gradually grew worse over the years and he began having real trouble fifteen years before the night he was prayed for. Here is his testimony recorded in a taped interview with Ken Tydeman.

Alan's Testimony

Fourteen months ago I came to the meeting for prayer. I had been hit on the neck with a rubber hose as a child and over the years deterioration had set in. Two young people I

met in the caravan park invited me to the meeting. I had given my life to Jesus several weeks before and that night I received the baptism of the Holy Spirit and spoke in tongues.

When I was prayed for I threw away my crutches as I felt the bones of my vertebrae move back into place. Previously my spine had an 's' shape and I also had trouble with one hip. From the moment of my healing I no longer needed the crutches, I threw them away. I've also had a wheel chair which I have not used since. In fact I sold it!

Before my healing I was taking 60 tablets a day for fifteen years, plus four mogadons at night, just for two hours sleep! I also had angina, and difficulty in breathing. The Lord healed me of these also fourteen months ago.

The only way I could sleep while I was ill was to cross one leg and draw both knees up until they touched my chin and lie partly on my stomach and half on one side. This was because of the spinal trouble and also because of the pain. Now I can stretch out completely. I was taking tablets for angina, and tablets for my breathing, as well as other medication. These cost me a hundred dollars every five months. They had no apparent effect, the pain was never eased, I had no relief twenty four hours a day. Now since my healing I have had no tablets, not even one for headache.

Tonight I was prayed for again because I had no feeling in my right leg from the toes to the knee, this also had been with me for fifteen years. I could be pricked with a pin and feel absolutely nothing. I now have complete feeling in my leg and indeed in my whole body. Jesus healed me, he is a miracle working God, nothing is impossible for him! (*Alan Jones*)

Scoliosis Healed

When I was about eleven years old I was first

The Wonder and the Mystery of Divine Healing
Alison Chant

diagnosed with scoliosis. I had back pain and my father started taking me to chiropractors. Neither chiropractors nor doctors could do much for scoliosis so I lived with pain most of the time. My back got worse over the years and the scoliosis was starting to cause degeneration in my spine. I had an 's' curve in my back, the top of the spine went one way and the lower back the other way. My back also had a slight curve outwards. I had limited movement when I turned my head as my neck had seized up. Even when I sat I had pain and I found it hard to sit still. The pain would radiate out to my hip, then down my left leg and into my foot. My knee joints would also hurt. I could barely walk and was walking with a limp. It wasn't very pleasant living like that.

The day you all prayed for me, you held my legs out and one was shorter than the other. As you prayed my legs lined up straight, and then you said for me to stand. I was used to having pain when I stood, and before my healing I would have a lot of pain when I put my left leg down. So I stood then put my leg down very cautiously. Miraculously I had no pain; and then you said to walk and, before, when I walked the pain would get more intense.

But I walked and I said, *"There is no pain."* I walked up and down the room in great excitement as I was totally free of pain. My husband, Glen, and my daughters, who were used to seeing my spine crooked, examined me later and saw that it was perfectly straight. I can do things now I haven't been able to do for a long time. My whole body is freed up, and my head can turn freely. Now I can do things I couldn't do before, I recently walked around Sydney Harbour and the Opera House with my husband. Jesus healed me, by his stripes I am healed! *(Iverna Olsen)*

Cataract Removed Through Prayer

In the *Deniliquin Pastoral Times,* Tuesday, June 25th it was reported by Tertia Brunsdon that Mrs Maree Bass was healed of a cataract over her right eye.

"I can see now. I can see again. And my eye doesn't hurt anymore."

These were the joyous words uttered by a woman who had been blind in her right eye. Mrs Maree Bass was one of the people who claimed to have been healed after evangelist Pastor Ken Tydeman, prayed for her in Deniliquin on Thursday night.

Mrs Bass said she had a cataract growing over her right eye.

"Doctors suggested surgery. But I believe in God and in his healing power," Mrs Bass said. *"I knew I would be healed when Pastor Tydeman laid his hands on me."*

Pastor Tydeman was in Deniliquin on a four days' healing crusade. Although he has seen miracles performed after praying for the ill, he claims he was only an instrument in God's hands.

"I am not the healer, God is," he said.

CHAPTER FIFTEEN

HEALING TODAY

What is God doing today in the healing ministry?

Healing Evangelism

We praise God for what he is doing through some of the healing evangelists around the world. However these men and women cannot claim more than a percentage of healings in meetings where many folk may not know or understand the need for them to have active faith in God and his healing promise. There is a limit to the work of the healing evangelist as many people who come to their meetings have no background to help them in maintaining their healing. During a campaign there is seldom time for adequate teaching on healing or on active faith versus temporary faith and because of this when the meetings are over many do lose the blessing they have gained. Those people who are encouraged to belong to a church which believes the healing message have more hope of keeping hold of the blessing God has given to them.

Healing Rooms

There is an alternative which is gaining far more healings and miracles than are possible in very large gatherings of people. This is in the restoration of the John G. Lake Healing Rooms that he conducted in Spokane, Washington in the early 1900's, where trained people were available on a daily basis to pray with anyone needing healing.

Lake sought God earnestly when his family began to die. He came to know of divine healing and mighty miracles began to occur among those of his family still living. One sister was literally raised from the dead. He then spent years in Africa where such mighty healings occurred as to amaze the world and hundreds of churches were planted.

He returned to Spokane, Washington, in the USA where 100,000 healings were recorded over a period of years. One wonderful healing concerned a girl with a tubercular leg. Lake was also instrumental in the healing of Gordon Lindsay, the founder of *Christ for the Nations*. Gordon had food poisoning and lost twenty five pounds in two weeks. Lake prayed every day for seven days before the healing came. [25]

At Lake's healing centres those who required healing were encouraged to return on a regular basis for prayer and many did return, time after time, until their healing was complete. A panel of doctors was set up to examine each and every healing that took place. Spokane became the healthiest city in America at that time.

There is definitely a correlation between praying on a regular basis for people, and seeing many more healings. Jesus gave a clue to this type of prayer:

He replied, I saw Satan fall like lightning from heaven. I have given you authority to trample on snakes and

---

[25] See *Bible Days are Here Again* pgs.185-190 for Gordon's full testimony.

scorpions and to overcome all the power of the enemy; nothing will harm you (Lu 10:18).

The idea of a steady trample gives us a picture of this kind of continual prayer, going on day after day that can win through to victory where one prayer may not be sufficient.

In America a few years ago Reverend George Runyan introduced me to the Healing Room set up under the umbrella of City Church Ministries, San Diego, of which he is the director. He explained to me how it is conducted.

The rooms are set up in the style of a waiting room, similar to a doctor's office. Appointments are made and the people who need healing come and wait their turn for prayer. There are several different rooms available, depending on how many trained workers are scheduled to pray for the sick.

The people who come for healing prayer fill in a card stating their problem and their desire for healing. The trained workers do not look at this card until they have first prayed and requested the Lord to show them anything this particular person needs to attend to before they are anointed with oil and prayed for as directed in James 5:14-15.

This method is excellent as the person seeking healing can, over a period of time,

1. Find out if anything in his or her life needs to be attended to, or repented of;

2. Learn about divine healing.

3. Learn all they need to know about how to activate their faith in God for divine healing;

4. Keep coming back for prayer until their healing is complete.

One lady I spoke to at the Healing Rooms while I was there had had an operation to fix a rod to her spine. She had been in pain for twenty two years and returned several times to have the anointing with oil and prayer before she was completely healed. *"Now,"* she told me, *"I have been without pain since my healing and I can bend down, which I could not do before."*

I was assured that all of the people who are prayed for have to be under a doctor's care so the medical fraternity has no problem with what is happening so far. Here is the promise given by those who are involved in the San Diego Healing Room.

> The Healing Rooms provide a loving, safe, confidential environment where you can come to receive healing prayer.
>
> Some are healed instantly by a miraculous touch from God. Others receive their healing progressively over a period of days, weeks, or months. We are committed to pray for you for as long as it takes, contending for your healing until you are completely well!
>
> We minister salvation, physical healing and emotional healing to the complete person (spirit,

soul and body).[26]

The Healing Room in the East County of San Diego has been so successful that Reverend Runyan is in the process of establishing another in the North County.

The San Diego Healing Room came into existence because the vision was caught in November 2000 from hearing a tape by Cal Pierce, *Preparing the Way*. Cal Pierce is founder of the present day Healing Rooms in Spokane, Washington, USA.

Since then Healing Rooms have been springing up all over the USA and in other countries.

One caution concerning this type of healing prayer is the need to be very careful in the choosing of the persons who are to be trained in praying for the sick.

Who is chosen to pray?

Our Healing Rooms team consists of one hundred Christians from more than forty churches in the San Diego region. The healing Rooms are rooms full of the love of God and his presence to heal physically, emotionally, mentally and spiritually through loving, gifted and committed servants of our Lord Jesus Christ.

A family atmosphere of love and unity permeates the

---

[26] Taken from the pamphlet advertising the San Diego Healing Rooms; Directors Dan and Sarah Shepler www.sandiegohealingrooms.com/

Healing Rooms, even though our home churches are as diverse as Assembly of God, Baptist, Foursquare, Nazarene, Presbyterian, Roman Catholic, Vineyard and various Independent Fellowships.

Each worker must have a release from their pastor to qualify, as well as an interview with the Directors. Then an intensive training process begins with a three month commitment to serving in the Healing Rooms. [27]

There is also another problem that can arise for those who want to be used in healing prayer. It comes from an article by Johanna Michaelsen:

Johanna became caught up gradually into occult practices because she did not know the Word of God sufficiently to keep her safe. She became involved with Pachita, a psychic surgeon in Mexico, but realising something was wrong with her experience she renounced her occult activities and recommitted her life to Christ in '72 while at Dr. Frances Shaeffer's study centre, L'Abri, Switzerland.

In her article she says that it should be well established that those who wish to use the gifts of the Holy Spirit should have no remnants of any New Age or psychic gifts from other sources. If they have had anything to do with the occult or cultic practices before coming to the Lord and having a born again experience, these occult gifts and their former associations must be renounced. They should

---

[27] Ibid.

not use any gift until they have spent one year or more in the Word of God, learning how to do things God's way through the gifts of the Holy Spirit.

She indicates that sometimes people with psychic ability can come into the Christian church and because of ignorance continue to use the gifts they have. Unless such new Christians are well taught, she says, they can be deceived by lying spirits and think they are using the gifts described as attributable to the Holy Spirit of God.

> Because of our eagerness to see the power of God at work, because of our hunger to see signs and wonders and miracles, many of us have become undiscerning and have embraced every ecstatic vision, every supernatural manifestation as from the hand of God. We have, ever so subtly, allowed our base to shift from the solid objective grounding of God's Word and have come instead to place our focus on our experience as the standard for our beliefs.
>
> I truly believe that those with occult backgrounds should wait a season before seeking and exercising any of the more "spectacular" gifts of the Spirit until they have matured in the grace and knowledge of the Lord [28]

Short Term Missions Trips

During the last century short term missions trips have

---

[28] Johanna Michaelsen, <u>Beware of Counterfeit Spiritual Gifts,</u> Ministries Magazine; Spring 1985; pg. 69.

become more and more popular with Christians who desire to serve Christ in foreign lands but who cannot for various reasons give their whole life to foreign missions as more conventional missionaries do. This has been an excellent way to introduce young people to ministry and has given them opportunity to witness for their faith and to pray for the sick.

While writing this book I was privileged to talk with pastor Kelvin Matthews of Waiuku, New Zealand who had just returned from a trip to Fiji with members of his church, both old and young. They were filled with excitement as they had witnessed the opening of the eyes of two blind people and also the healing of a Hindu man who was in hospital with leukaemia. This man was near death when prayed for but soon left the hospital completely healed. He returned home to throw out and destroy all of his idols and to accept the Lord as his Saviour. The short term missionaries saw many other healings as well during their weeks in Fiji. This kind of encounter is very strengthening to the faith of Christian people who normally do not see the Word of God working in their home land so dramatically.

The Local Church

The experience of the local church has always been that some are healed. If the healing message is preached in faith, in season and out of season, and the faith of the people is raised by ongoing miracles then we should see even more healing. Miracles are happening! May they increase as we study the healing message, seek God for answers as to why some are not healed, and believe God for yet more marvellous answers to believing prayer.

CHAPTER SIXTEEN

CONCLUSIONS

The Lord never requires us to wait for him to do what we can well do for ourselves. If we are in need of finance we do not sit under a palm tree asking him for funds to fall from heaven. No, if we have common sense we will ask him to help us find the means to earn the money or raise it through some other human means.

If we need direction we indicate our willingness to be in his will and then we ask him to lead us through the circumstances which come our way.

If we need healing our first understanding needs to be that all healing comes from God. If we are Christians, believing in divine healing and the power of God, then he expects us to live in such a way, by eating correctly, exercising, and avoiding those things that will poison us, so that health and well being will permeate our physical bodies.

If we do need prayer, healing can come to us gradually or God can accelerate the natural healing of our physical body. The Lord can heal in other ways too; through our doctor's advice and prescription, through surgery, or various therapies. Although ideally, the way God has formed us; depending on our ancestry and the availability of good food and plenty of exercise, our bodies are built to heal themselves.

God has created help for our physical body through his natural creation. Healing is then a blessing from God that comes through the natural healing processes he has gifted us with, coupled with our faith in his goodness toward us.

We are taught also that our whole being, spirit, soul and body can be kept whole and healthy through the taking of communion in the correct manner. As we trust the Lord to forgive our sins and cleanse us from all unrighteousness (1 Jn 1:8-9) our emotions are stabilised and the joy of the Lord fills us daily. We are truly made whole and complete as we seek to please the Lord in all we do.

Sickness Called Discipline

It seems clear from 1 Corinthians 11:23-32 that we can become sick by not discerning the Lord's body correctly and that this sickness is called discipline (verse 32): but if so, then the remedy is available to us, and through repentance we can be restored.

If through inheritance of family genes, or ignorance in knowing how to live properly, we become sick for some reason that is not clear to us then we can still seek the Lord for healing. He has promised this in the Old Testament (Is 53:5) and he has repeated the promise in the New Testament (1 Pe 2:24). Because of this promise we can ask the Lord for the blessing of healing and also for him to guide the doctor we have consulted that he might treat us successfully.

Christians who keep their faith strong will be in a much better position to believe God than a half-hearted Christian who has neglected the means of grace - Bible study, prayer, fellowship, communion and witness. We can increase our faith in healing by reading and meditating on the healing scriptures and by reading about other people who have experienced the healing power of God.

If healing is taught consistently and courageously then the faith of the people who hear these faith building sermons will rise, and every victory will increase their faith. If enough Christians grasp hold of the potential power in the Word of God then healing will become more evident. If the surrounding community becomes aware of what God can do, then even more wonderful miracles can begin to occur.

If the person being prayed for is a non-Christian and is earnestly seeking God's healing power then there may be no blockage to their healing. God is a good God and he is gracious in his dealings with the ignorant. But, if people do not then accept Jesus as Saviour and prefer to go on in their sinful way of life, not acknowledging God's blessing, then their sickness could return, or a worse sickness could come on them. Jesus said to the man at the Pool of Bethesda, *"See, you are well again. Stop sinning or something worse may happen to you."*

Those who are already Christians should be looking to the Lord to bless them with health and strength as they take hold of the means of grace. If they should become sick for any reason then the way is open for them to call for the elders of the church, seek God for a reason for their sickness, be it physical or spiritual, and ask for forgiveness if necessary.

There may be a sin they need to repent of, as mentioned in the ministry of Alexander Dowie, or there may be something God wants to show them before he heals them, or it is not God's time for them to experience a miracle. There may be something he wants to show them before he grants such a boon. Or it may be that they have reached their three score years and ten and this is the sickness that will take them home to be with the Lord.

Divine Healing Needs Wisdom.

People should not be forced to claim their healing if they are not ready and no one should be despised for not having enough faith. Great wisdom is needed in the healing ministry so that it is not brought into disrepute.

God has promised healing but he has not promised to perform miracles every time we ask for one.

For a paraplegic to walk again a miracle of the regrowth of nerves would have to be granted.

I have a dear friend, Mary, who was unfortunate enough to contract poliomyelitis when only two and a half years of age. She learned about divine healing power when in her fortieth year, and would have loved to glorify God with a miracle of regrowth of nerves so that she could walk again. Although initially she felt sure this would happen the miracle was not granted her and for many years she felt it was her fault that she had not been able to walk. Many well meaning Christians prayed for her and exhorted her to believe God and get up and walk. These persons left her feeling let down and miserable. However, she shook off these emotions and refused to let her condition hold her back from serving the Lord. Walking with her heavy callipers, special boots, and her crutch and stick she spent four years in Africa as a missionary secretary to an eye doctor. Now she hosts a prayer and Bible study in her home and still teaches piano in her eighty fifth year. She has done much with little and puts many able-bodied Christians to shame for their lack of zeal!

In contrast to healing, miracles come at different times through various ministries. They come more frequently where God is confirming his Word in a heathen country, or when he has given a special gift, or granted a special period of time when his healing power will move in a powerful way.

Sometimes a word of knowledge is given. This does stimulate faith in people as they suddenly realise God loves them, knows who they are, and knows what is their particular problem. This can be very moving to a person who has perhaps had some doubts about God's personal love and care. This happened in the healing of Mrs Harvey and Mrs French as depicted in chapter one of this book.

If you look at the lives of Elijah and of Elisha there were not a lot of miracles recorded in their ministries over the period of their life time. Those miracles they did have were truly amazing and wonderful but there are eight only recorded for Elijah and sixteen for Elisha, who was promised twice the blessing afforded Elijah. These two lived under the Old Testament healing promise for the people of Israel yet, according to the written Word, were not called upon to pray for many of them. (1 Kg 17:1 – 2Kg 13:20)

A Realm of Faith!

There are some who have been given a special gift of healing and who move in a realm of faith that is remarkable, such as Pastors Ken and Marjorie Tydeman, already featured in this book. When a man, a woman, who moves in the healing gift, speaks a word of faith under the anointing of God, they know that the healing is already accomplished. Faith is created in the hearts of the hearers and God moves to grant a miracle, as in the case of Frank Holland.

There have been many others, caught up by God and anointed for a special ministry of healing. In the last century Maria Woodworth Etter, John G. Lake, Gordon Lindsay, Jack Coe, and Oral Roberts; in the USA; George Jeffries, and Wigglesworth in England; Alexander Dowie (who later moved to USA), Leo Harris, and C. L. Greenwood in Australia, and there have been many more too numerous to mention.

Apart from these more famous names there have been many unsung heroes, quiet pastors who have believed God and seen miracles among their people, which have never been publicised.

Why has there been this enormous upsurge of God's healing power in this generation.

There are two reasons.

First, the proliferation of healings has occurred because of the outpouring of the Holy Spirit and the many millions who have received this baptism of power in the past one hundred years. This baptism brought with it a new understanding of the gifts of the Spirit and their potential.

Second, because there has been a fresh revelation of the new creation message and of the authority we have been given by the Lord to proclaim his gospel to the world.

But there is a need to understand the healing message and its boundaries and some I have discussed in this book. I have endeavoured first to understand and then to convey to you some of the mysteries of the healing promise.

Sometimes we forget that, *"Precious in the eyes of the Lord is the death of his saints"(Ps 116:15)*. We cannot live for ever! The ideal is for us to live a healthy life and die, full of years, by going to sleep in the Lord, without any major sickness invading our body.

Unfortunately, because of the man-made poisons that are in this world this is an ideal that not many of us can expect. However we can look forward to our new body, which will be like Jesus resurrection body, unable to take sick ever again! Praise God.

A Challenge!

I would like to present a challenge to the new generation of Christians rising up to preach the gospel today. That is to take up the promise of God and to preach healing, in season and out of season, until we begin to see the mighty healing power of God moving in our land, inspiring those who are unbelievers to believe in our God who can work wonders.

The Wonder and the Mystery of Divine Healing
Alison Chant

APPENDIX

Prepare the way for your deliverance with these powerful scriptures!

On the Believer's Authority
Luke 10:9; Revelation 12:10-11; Acts 10:38; Philippians 4:13

On the Assurance of Sins Forgiven
Isaiah 1:18; 1 John 1:9; Romans 10:9-13

On submission to the Will of God
James 4:7; Romans 12:1-2

On the Power of Jesus' Name
Mark 16:17; Philippians 2:9-12; Acts 3:6, 16; John 16:24

On Your Legal Position with Christ
Ephesians 2:4-6; Colossians 1:27; 2:10; Romans 6:11

On the Power of the Word of God
John 8:32; Ephesians 6:17; Hebrews 4:12

On casting out Demons
Mark 16:17; Acts 8:7; James 4:7; 1 Peter 5:7-11

On Your Right to Freedom
Luke 4:18; Acts 26:18; Galatians 5:1; Colossians 1:13-14

On the Strength of Christ Within You
Romans 8:31; 2 Corinthians 2:14; 9:8; Ephesians 6:10; 1:19-20; 3:20; Philippians 4:13; Colossians 1:11, 27; 2:13-15

On the Power of a Right Confession
Romans 10:9; Hebrews 3:1; Romans 4:17-21

On the Ministry of the Holy Spirit
2 Timothy 1:7; 2 Corinthians 3:17-18.

How to gain the most benefit from these scriptures.

You should copy the above scriptures from your Bible, and then write them out again in your own words.
Personalise them. Put your own name into them. Write them in a way that relates them to your particular circumstance and need.
Pray over them. Open yourself to them. Keep on working with them until they become powerfully alive in your spirit (Ephesians 1:17-20).
Thus you will build a foundation of spiritual authority upon which you can both gain and retain a striking victory over the works of the enemy!

Strengthen your faith for healing with these Scriptures

Old Testament

Ex 15:22-26; Psalm 30:2; 103:1-5;107:20; Pr 3:7-8; 4:20-22; 12:18; 16:24; Is 53:5; Mal 4:2;

New Testament

Mt 4:23-25; Mt 8:5-10; 9:1-8, 18-33; Mt 10: 5-8; 12:9-13; Mt 14:13-14; Mk 5:21-43; 5:17-26; 9:10-11; 10:46-52; 11:22-25; Lu 5:17-26; 8:40-56; 9:1-41; 13:10-13; 14:1-4; 17:11-17; 18:35-43; Jn 4:46-54; 5:1-15; 14:9-14; Acts 3:1-10; 14:8-10; 28:7-10; Ro 10:17; 1 Co 12:7-11; He 10:35-38; 11:1; Ja 5:13-16; 1 Pe 2:24; 3 Jn:2.

BIBLIOGRAPHY:

Ken Chant, Healing in the Old Testament, Vision Publishing; Ramona. CA. USA. 2005.

Ken Chant, Healing in the New Testament, Vision Publishing. Ramona. CA. USA. 2005.

Ken Chant, Faith Dynamics, Vision Bible College. Sydney. Australia 1976.

Ken Chant, Throne Rights, Vision Bible College. Sydney. Australia 1976.

Gordon Lindsay, Bible Days are Here Again, Shreveport, LA. USA 1949.

F.F. Bosworth, Christ the Healer, Fleming H. Revell Co. Old Tappan, New Jersey. USA 1973.

Francis McNutt, Healing, Ave Maria Press Edition. 1974.

Gordon Lindsay (Ed.), The New John G. Lake Sermons. Published by "Christ for the Nations", Dallas, TX. USA.

Kenneth Copeland (Ed.), John G. Lake – His Life, His Sermons, His Boldness of Faith, Kenneth Copeland Publications. Fort Worth, TX. USA. 1994.

Don Colbert, Toxic Relief, M. D. Siloam; A. Strang Co. Lake Mary, FL. USA. 2001

Ray Bloomfield, It's Not a Sin to Be Sick But it's Very Nice to Be Well, Here's How, Ken Duncan Panographs.1996. Printed by Griffin Paperbacks, Netley. South Australia.

The Wonder and the Mystery of Divine Healing
Alison Chant

www.ingramcontent.com/pod-product-compliance
Lightning Source LLC
Chambersburg PA
CBHW031628160426
43196CB00006B/323